The author is born and bred in Scotland of English lineage. He has interest in art, cars, boats and biology. He was ambitious to become a pilot, farmer, medical vet and a scientist. Fate dictated direction after serving in NCB and learning to fly with Royal Navy. An ear infection ended his flying career, so he entered medical field and then vet labs. He obtained master's degree in immunology. He married a nurse and moved career into quality assurance consultancy. He published booklets on 'Isla' and cartoon booklet on general cancer. So far in his life, he has lived actively with cancer for 19 years.

Best Wishes,

Haydon Jeffery.

I dedicate this book to my wife (Nee) Louise Pavier Hughes who has spent 19 years of our marriage tolerating my condition with prostate cancer, heart attack, stroke, 32 days of radiotherapy, chemotherapy and effects of medication. My wife has contributed to my recovery which is a miracle with occasional lapses. I also believe that animals have healing powers. Isla, our spaniel, aided my recovery for 14 years until old age dictated termination of her life. I am now 81 years old.

Francis Hayden Jeffery

OPERATION UPSET

AUSTIN MACAULEY PUBLISHERS™

LONDON • CAMBRIDGE • NEW YORK • SHARJAH

A CIP catalogue record for this title is available from the British Library.

ISBN 9781528984843 (Paperback)
ISBN 9781528984850 (Hardback)
ISBN 9781528984867 (ePub e-book)

www.austinmacauley.com

First Published (2021)
Austin Macauley Publishers Ltd
25 Canada Square
Canary Wharf
London
E14 5LQ

I greatly appreciate Verity Walker's recommendation to contact David Spooner—known to have skill in fast, accurate typing with laser printer and ability to upload text and illustrations for publishing. Constructive discussion was also held with author, Elizabeth Sutherland, in order to expedite the path to publication of *Operation Upset*.

Introduction

Old English (No 700), Male

New Zealand (No 605). Female

The sun was shining brightly through the skylight windows
by courtesy of the controlling humans. The animals were fully

aware that humans dominated the environment, food, animal slavery, experiments, labour, pets and occupation of land, sea and air (weather permitting). Anyway, frustration was broken by the rabbits' hind legs thumping on their cage floors. Lack of space within the cages was too much for some, who found it necessary to indulge in a mini-marathon, round and round, thump, thump at every turn. Then silence, boredom and I suppose despair.

The animals frequently ear-wigged, listening in to discussions between the sub-contractors who routinely cleaned the animal house. The partners were much-travelled ex-military dog or horse handlers. One discussion really disturbed the inmates when they overheard accounts of the way some elephants abroad had been 'broken' as part of the training to be obedient to humans. They had witnessed elephants being firmly 'boxed' within tight and primitive cages to prevent movement or retaliation. A handler would sit on the back of the elephant and frequently hit it on the head with a spiked implement to control any disallowed movement or reaction. Intelligent elephants soon got the message. The cleaners also voiced opinion on dogs being bred for human consumption abroad. Up to 20 dogs per cage, each selected for removal (and death), as required, by use of a long-handled claw device closed around the neck of the dog, then clubbed.

Farm animals in the western world are looked after but only to benefit humans and to gain higher prices at market. Humans seem to be at the better end of existence and the food chain.

Conversation was the mainstay of survival in the rabbit room but was on a quieter level than among the guinea-pigs housed up the corridor. The chatter and chitter created by 'The Pigs' was akin to a WVS seminar during coffee breaks, only to be broken when a waitress drops a loaded tray of sandwiches and tea. The silence, being only very brief, which in turn is then restarted by the female vocals, verbally accelerating to full crescendo, as if nothing had happened.

Why do the delegates stop talking, turn and look? It must be obvious what has happened and because it is not life-threatening, why bother to be distracted? Any sudden noise will silence the guinea-pigs in exactly the same way. I suppose it indicates the partial evolution of humans from the furry coated state to the relatively bald end product.

Chapter 1
The Animal House

"Hello, Old English. How are you today?"

"I'm not so bad, New Zealand white. Not so bad at all."

"What was all the activity last night? I don't mind the occasional thump but that was ridiculous!"

"Oh, I think the Polish giant along the end was feeling a bit off colour. They have been watching him for the last day or two. I think he was taken away this morning. We won't see him again."

"Why not?" asked Old English.

"Well, they're pretty intolerant toward sick bunnies around here, you know. Bad for business so they say. In fact, it is better for us too, you know, because we are less likely to get an infection."

"Yes, I suppose you're right," said Old English.

"To change the subject, New Zealand, how old are you?"

"A very dangerous age you could say, Old English. A very dangerous age indeed!"

"Why do you say that, New Zealand?"

"Well, old pal, that's the age when most of us are boxed off."

"What do you mean, boxed off? Really, you are a comic at times."

"You've got to be a comic to survive this life," said New Zealand. "Seriously, it means being put in to a cardboard box and being sent off to a place where they do experiments. 5,385,575 animals were used last year."

"Experiments?" quizzed Old English. "What kind of experiments?"

"Who knows, nobody ever returns to tell the tale," said New Zealand.

"Oh God!" cried Old English. "Doesn't sound too good to me."

"Nor to me," exclaimed New Zealand. "But that's one possible future for both of us whether we like it or not."

"You mean that we are offered alternative fates!" cried Old English. He was now beginning to panic at the prospect of getting an answer that displeased him yet again.

"Well," said New Zealand. "You could be sold as a pet to a good home, or – New Zealand paused, having sensed Old English's apprehension – you could be sold to a bad home, or for dog meat, or the ultimate honour: For human consumption."

"The odds of ending up in a utopia are rather slim," said Old English.

"That's right," agreed New Zealand. "The 'lot' of a rabbit is not a happy lot, old bun."

"You seem to accept your lot," said Old English.

"Well, we are looked after here and I suppose we will be looked after equally well if used for research. I only hope that death is quick if I end up as a potential meal," said New Zealand.

"Oh God!" wept Old English. "Don't tell me any more, please!"

"I'm sorry," said New Zealand. "But you did ask."

At that moment the big wooden door at the end of the large rabbit house was moved to one side and in walked the animal breeder's staff. It was 9 am and time for checking the water supply and food hoppers. A breath of cool, fresh air blew through the animal house, chasing out the hot and humid air that always collected. The rabbits became excited at the presence of humans and the invigorating air.

They could also sense something else. A large van was parked outside. The driver was looking at a large list of tabulated weights and rabbit breeds. He supported the clipboard on his fat, beery belly and squinted through curly eyebrows. He looked comical at 5'3" with his blue trousers barely supported by his thighs at one end and his black safety boots at the other. His waist served no function here.

According to the dark logo on his T-shirt, *he* was Tarzan (in between and beneath the tea stains). Presumably, he had a habit of emptying his flask enroute. Either that or he had a leak in his mouth. New Zealand mused at the thought of him drinking so much tea that it overflowed from his ears on to his T-shirt.

"What is he about to do?" asked Old English.

"Oh, he is about to select his rabbits for delivery," replied New Zealand. "But I thought we were not going to discuss the matter any further?"

"Of course, of course," said Old English. "I'm terribly sorry."

"Not at all," cried New Zealand. "Glad to oblige, but it really won't help you."

The driver came in to the house and glanced at the labels on the cages. The labels contained the animals' date of birth, sex, strain, approximate weight etc.

The driver began to make his selection.

New Zealand knew that it would only be a matter of time before Old English started to ask more questions, so she thought it would be easier on herself if she just started to give a commentary.

She told Old English to look at the rabbit which had just been selected for removal. "That poor devil is destined for the food pot," she said. "Looks the right weight to me!"

"Better to remain skinny," retorted Old English.

"Quite so, quite so," remarked New Zealand. "If it is any consolation, my own strain is the most popular for eating because we are usually very well-built. A good feed, as you might say!"

"Thank God," said a much-relieved Old English.

"Unfortunately," exclaimed New Zealand, "we are also firm favourites with the experimenters. I did hear a rumour that it had something to do with having big ears but I don't know whether it is true."

"If that were the case," began Old English, "surely half-lop and his like, over there, would be of more use to them?"

"Quite right, my friend. Quite right, indeed. You are a most observant bun!"

"Thank you, kind friend. Thank you," said Old English.

"Oh, by the way. If it is any consolation, I would imagine that you will end up as a family pet because of your attractive black and white markings. In particular the butterfly mark on your nose."

"Do you really think so?" asked Old English, brightening up.

"Oh yes, indeed," remarked New Zealand with an air of reassurance. Her confident answer completely pacified her nervous colleague.

"New Zealand!" shouted Old English. "What is the dangerous age that you spoke about earlier on?"

"Four months," replied New Zealand.

Old English gasped in shock. He was almost that age!

"Have no fear, my friend," said New Zealand. "Trust in what I have told you. Have faith in your colour and appearance. A pet I am sure you will be."

Deep down Old English wasn't really convinced. He wished that he could conjure up just one speck of New Zealand's confidence. Perhaps he was the wrong type of bun to be confident under such circumstances?

Perhaps in the next world, if there is one, he will be a more confident strain of bun, just like New Zealand. Or better still, a human being.

How lucky human beings seem to be, he thought. *Although, I suppose they must have some problems even if it is only the problem of selecting the right bun for the right purpose.*

It seemed a silly world, really! Without humans they would all be free. A little colder and hungrier, but free nevertheless. Actually, the thought of nice lush grass made his mouth water. They only got dry old pellets to eat most of the time. All very nourishing, admittedly, provided you ate them. On reflection, if might be a good idea to diet from now on to avoid the cooking pot.

Suddenly, the driver of the van seemed to be looking for 'Old English' strains.

All his brothers and sisters seemed to be sitting in cardboard boxes read for transportation.

Chapter 2
In the Van

Old English felt horrible. He was sure he was next. The cage door was opened by the driver and a massive hand forced its way in to the cage. Old English dashed to one side of his cage and then to the other. The driver got impatient, knelt down to get a better view and made a very quick grab for the rabbit. He was very experienced at catching rabbits in cages, following Old English around the cage and making quick grabs at the scruff of the creature's neck. It was only a matter of time before OldEnglish would be 'boxed', as New Zealand might say.

Sure enough, a big hand came down at the correct moment and floored Old English. The fingers of the driver closed about his fur. He was as good as in the box.

He overheard the driver utter to himself, "Cohen's Pet Shop on the corner." Old English breathed a sigh of relief. Surely, he would now be alright for the rest of his natural life. Come to think of it, there wasn't anything natural about living in a cage. He had to laugh, though, to put himself in the right frame of mind for the future.

He turned to have a last look at New Zealand. He wondered what would happen to her. Old English had a funny feeling that things were not going to be good for his friend.

The driver lined up the boxes in pairs and carried two in each hand towards the waiting van. He gently placed the living parcels on the floor of the vehicle and slid them towards those which had already been positioned.

Old English looked out of the air hole in the box and noticed that there was room in the van for a further six boxes.

He quietly hoped that New Zealand would occupy one of those spaces.

The driver went off for his coffee break before starting his day's deliveries. The van became suddenly quiet, but for the occasional creak from the suspension and exhaust, which contracted as it cooled. Some of the bucks showed their annoyance at having been disturbed by banging the floor with their hind feet. It sounded like someone wielding a hammer. The bun in the box next to Old English began to sneeze. He had a touch of snuffles, something Old English knew to be contagious. He hoped that the van driver would come back to check his load and remove the smitten colleague. He knew of course that this final inspection was unlikely to take place now that they were all boxed and ready to go. How careless of him not to notice the nasal discharge when he first loaded the animal! Who knows how many fellow rabbits would now be infected in the future?

The driver eventually returned, climbed in to his cab, started the engine, put it in to gear with a bit of a graunch and began to move off. He was just passing the office when the secretary came rushing out with a piece of paper in her hand. It was another rather belated order. The van driver pulled up, steering the van towards the secretary's feet in a mock attempt to run her over. They both laughed.

"Bloody idiot!" cried a New Zealand doe who had, up until that time, been quietly snoozing away in her box.

They heard some rumblings about rabbits being needed for that research place up the road. Sure enough, the van reversed – or rather, rocketed – back to the rabbit house. The handbrake was carelessly applied before the van had stopped. It was the driver's party trick, which he had honed to a fine art. The van stopped, as always, right outside the door of the rabbit house. The driver jumped out and entered the house, selected four New Zealand whites, placed them in to the van and re-entered the building. He stood and looked around for a further two specimens. He spotted Old English's acquaintance, the New Zealand, lifted her up and – having satisfied himself as to her suitability – placed her in a box. He proceeded to make the total up to six and locked the van door.

The occupants of the van now knew that this would definitely be the last time that they would see the animal breeders' premises.

"Haven't got rid of me yet!" exclaimed a familiar voice. Old English could not believe his ears.

"Is that you, New Zealand?" he cried.

"None other, my old friend!" she replied. "It is only I, in the fur. Only I, sir!"

Old English was pleased and yet a little sad that his colleague had joined him on the mystery tour. He cast his mind back to the possible destinations and fates awaiting them. Old English noticed that he had been placed next to the door of the van. He assumed that he would be one of the first to be delivered, so to speak. He had always imaged that his deliverance would be something more regal.

Obviously, the realities of the outside world are different to the contrivances of the rabbit mind.

After some time, the van came to a halt in a large and noisy main street. The van driver opened the door, lifted out several boxes of lupine activity and closed the door. It all happened so quickly. New Zealand had been taken out of the van with the others.

Old English had barely had time to shout a farewell. And anyway, wasn't it he that was destined for the pet shop?

New Zealand found herself on the pavement outside Cohen's Pet Shop. Her new life was about to begin in earnest but she was confused. From what she had gathered the New Zealand breeds rarely made it to the pet shops. She shouted a good-bye to Old English, hoping that he would hear above the noise of the traffic.

Old English didn't reply. He obviously hadn't heard New Zealand's call over the hubbub.

Eventually the van drove off, leaving the rabbits safely in the hands of the pet shop owner. New Zealand soon found herself sitting in the window of the shop. She wasn't sure if it was a mistake or fate that had brought her here but she considered herself lucky to have avoided a more unpleasant outcome after leaving the breeding house.

All she desired now was a comfortable home, though she hoped very much that Old English would fare well wherever he ended up.

The van was by now well in to the day's deliveries. Old English was still on board and by this time feeling rather uncomfortable in his cardboard box. He was still shocked by the sudden departure of New Zealand. He hardly had room to turn around and could only see out with difficulty. The movement of the noisy van was causing him a lot of distress and at certain speeds the high-frequency vibrations were really quite painful. Humans were apt to build vans for human comfort and not for the comfort of hairy rabbits, or even bald ones for that matter.

The van slipped off the motorway – or rather, skidded off as it was getting near to the driver's finishing time – and came to a halt three miles down the road. They had arrived at a pharmaceutical firm's premises. The driver spoke to the security guard, who allowed him to drive his van across to the animal house. The animal house staff must have heard the van as it arrived because they suddenly appeared at the door. The van was duly unloaded, then went on its way back to where it had departed from earlier.

Chapter 3
The Medical Research Place

The rabbits were lifted inside the animal house and transferred to wire cages which were positioned along the walls of a room marked *Quarantine*. Old English looked around his new home. This wasn't a pet shop, that was for sure. The floors were soaking wet and there was a distinct smell of disinfectant. Clearly, the floors had just been hosed down. Although the room was air-conditioned the air was very humid and the smell of disinfectant, though strong, did not mask the smell of the rats and mice which Old English had noticed in cages in another room. The air conditioning was clearly of an inferior type, one that tended to mix the air from adjoining rooms together. The noise of the fans caused a background noise which Old English knew would be annoying. It was probably one of those things that a caged bun would be obliged to tolerate. So much for peace and quiet in his new domain.

Old English had twenty-four roommates in all. Some had just arrived but most were under the attention of the vet for minor infections and wounds. He could not help noticing that on each cage there was a card which contained the same information that had been printed on the cards at the animal breeders. In addition, each card was numbered. This number was in fact the number assigned to the animal within the cage. It became obvious that Old English was going to be called number 700. He was quietly amused at the observation that 700 is the reverse of 007, the number associated with a rather randy human 'rabbit' made famous by the cinema, or so he was led to believe from overheard discussions between animal house staff. At that moment Old English could not visualise getting the opportunity to be randy so perhaps a number which was the reverse of 007 would make a more fitting name for his future after all.

Across the room, Old English – or rather, 700 – could see number 605. She was a massive full-grown rabbit. Another New Zealand white! A pang of sadness tugged at Old English's little heart. He wished he'd had a chance to say good bye to his old companion properly.

"How long have you been here?" asked the newly-named 700.

"Too bloody long," she retorted.

"Had a hard time, then?"

"My legs are killing me," she replied. "Been sitting here in these damned cages for about a year. Never get any real exercise, cages are too small you know. *Home Office approved* though, they are! The bloody inspector who passed these cages needs to spend a night in here with me. Soon change his evil little mind, I would. Home Office approved indeed! Needs bloody glasses!"

"Eeeh, you do go on," cried 700. "But I can understand. I'm sure I will be the next one to complain. I like my room, too. Must get moving about during the day. What are you in quarantine for anyway, 605?"

"Oh, I had a swelling on my cheek. The vet removed it for me. He's a good old boy, really. Won't let you suffer, you know. Soon tells 'em off if he finds out that they have been inattentive. They are usually very good, though. Wouldn't put up with the job if they weren't keen. Real animal lovers they are. Usually a happy lot, too. Never heard any arguments yet. The lab staff on the other hand are often having a go. Too much rivalry there. Different sort of folk all together. Still, it wouldn't do for us all to be the same."

"You don't seem to miss much."

"Not much else to do all day except observe," replied 605. "Could have done a lot with my time had I been a human. Can't do much with four feet in place of two feet and two hands, though."

700 laughed. "You are a scream!"

"A brain the size of a hen's egg doesn't help either."

"You are in a bad way!"

"A moan now and again does no harm," replied 605 with a smile.

"What do they use you for?" asked 700.

"Who, me? Oh, I'm honoured. I'm used for their supply of non-immune rabbit serum," said 605 rather proudly. "Guarantees long life around here."

"Long life? Like one of those torch batteries?" asked 700 with an impish sense of humour.

"Aye, just like that lad, except that I might not be classified as hazardous waste. I'm a good bleeder in many ways, am I."

"What do you think will happen to me?" asked 700, realising that the future was currently just one big question.

"Oh, I don't know," replied 605. "Could end up like me I suppose or they could immunise you with something. Or they could—"

"Wait, wait," said 700, butting in. "Wait a minute here. What is immunise? What does that word mean? It sounds positively awful."

"Well, old son, they usually inject some concoction in to you in the hope that you will produce an antibody response."

"Hey now, that's enough of that talk 605. I'm going to go and see my union about this. They can't just inject me! I'm damned if I'll let them off with such a thing."

"Won't get much choice, I'm afraid. When they grab you, you have to take what's coming."

"Bloody Hell, 605. I most certainly don't!"

"Well, I suppose you can always bite them," said 605. "But it will only delay things and may even lead to your premature death if they think you're badly behaved. They don't like rabbits that bite."

"Oh, damn you, 605. I am not here for the good of my health so I'm going to fight!"

"Please yourself, 700. I can only advise you. Perhaps it is easier for me. We all have different temperaments."

One of the animal house staff entered the room, looked around and saw that everything was all right before leaving again. Judging from the noise of doors opening and closing throughout the facility 700 reasoned that he must be doing a final inspection of the premises before closing up.

Sure enough, 605 verified that was the final ritual of the day. The main door was heard to shut and the animal house was suddenly quiet. At least, it was as quiet as it would ever be with the confounded fans blowing all night. In fact, talking of nuisances, 700 had become consciously aware of a small but annoying draught. It was emanating from a duct in the ceiling above his cage.

So much for man's inventions, he thought to himself.

The night passed very quietly and with little activity other than the occasional sneeze and bang. Even during the night some rabbits saw reason to stamp their hind feet against the bottom of their cage. Others had a quiet nibble at the rather dry old pellets of food. It was the general opinion among the long-eared fraternity that the man who invented food in the form of pellets should be shot. *How far removed could you get from nice, lush greens? They were darned expensive too, so they had heard. Still, those costs serve them right for making us slaves,* thought the rabbits.

Chapter 4
Prepare to Meet Thy Doom

About two weeks later a scientist came in to the quarantine room and marked the cards of six of the rabbits. Number 700 had his card marked with a person's name and asked 605 what was going on.

"Getting ready for another experiment, I suppose," answered 605. "You will have to wait, however, before you find out what kind of experiment it is going to be."

"I suddenly feel uneasy," said 700 with a slightly nervous tone.

"I can understand that. Never get used to it myself, although I'm pretty safe. I think. Better not to think too deeply old boy. Crunch a pellet during such times. I do, that's one reason why I am so big and fat!"

"I'm too nervous to eat a single thing," replied 700. "But thanks all the same. I am glad you are around to help."

"Sorry I can't do more, old sport, but the way things are I'm kind of caged-in. Wish we were out in the wild right now. Wouldn't half show the blighters where to go with their needles."

"Needles?" shouted 700 in surprise. "What bloody needles!? Nobody mentioned anything about needles to me before I came here. Good God, woman, you must be having me on."

"No, sir," replied 605 confidently. "Me no jokey about such things."

"Well, I am going to fight," said 700, gathering his determination. "I've made up my mind. The more I think about this whole sordid saga the worse it gets."

"Quite true. That is why I told you earlier not to think about it. It doesn't help one bit."

"I don't suppose you can tell me any details of the experiments, can you?" asked 700.

"No sirree Baahb, I ain't gonna tell yer out else," said 605 in an American accent.

"Okay, well to change the subject: Where did you get that accent from?"

"Oh, I often impersonate the scientists who come in here," replied 605. "Makes a light-hearted change now and again."

700's mind soon forgot the humour and returned to the major worry of the moment. Obviously, he would have to wait for events to give him the answer to his many unasked questions.

He did not have to wait long to get his answers. A rather hefty young lass came striding in to the room, opened the door of 700's cage and inserted her hand. Judging by her confident attitude she fully expected to gather up a willing bundle of rabbit, but as we already know, 700 had other ideas.

He ran around the cage several times in quick succession before finally settling in to a corner. Here he sat with his rump firmly wedged in one corner. He furiously stamped his feet, licked his lips and prepared for action. The girl bent down to get a better view inside the cage, reinserted her hand and moved it towards 700's scruff. 700 let fly with all his might. He raised himself on to his rear legs as high as he was able to in the Home Office approved cage and took a flying leap at the girl's outstretched hand. His incisors sank in to her hand as if it belonged to an attacking ferret. He was out to affirm the misconception that rabbits do not bite and are rarely aggressive.

There was a loud shriek from the girl, who ran out of the room with blood pouring from a nasty-looking wound. Some minutes later she returned with one of the male members of staff. She pointed a rather punctured finger at 700 and uttered, "That's the one! The swine!"

700 had never been called a swine before. He wasn't sure that he liked it all that much. "Bloody cheek," he muttered. "No manners these days."

At that moment, 700 could not see any fault in his own actions. He was, as before, convinced that he was right. He had every intention of living with his decision to retaliate. To be quite honest, it looked to an onlooker as if 700 would probably die as a result of his decision.

"Bloody thing will have to go!" he heard the girl yell.

Her colleague laughed. "Off males now, are you?" he said.

"Oh, shut up, you idiot," she replied. "Get the beast out of the cage before I shoot it."

By this time the other members of staff had arrived to witness the spectacle of 700 being removed from his cage. He suddenly felt embarrassed by the publicity. Number 605, who had remained quiet for some time, shouted her support for poor old 700.

"Thanks, friend!" replied 700. "Any support at this time is of help. Thanks very much!"

The man who had arrived to help the girl in her hour of need put on a thick glove and very confidently grabbed 700 by the ears, dragged him to the front of the cage, placed his ungloved hand behind 700 and lifted him in to the crook of his arm.

700 lay there quietly with his nose snuggled in to his sleeve. The green jacket he was wearing smelled as though it was fresh from the laundry. He had to admit he was really quite comfortable, certainly in comparison to sitting on wire flooring.

The man bore no malice. In fact, he began to stroke 700 in an effort to comfort him. 700 began to wonder how he would be treated if he was in the arms of the irate girl. The thought put a shudder down his spine.

The man in the green jacket carried 700 out of the room, down the corridor and in to a room labelled 'Bleeding Room'.

As far as 700 was concerned all rooms in that place, on that morning, were 'Bleeding Rooms' in more than one sense!

Chapter 5
The Bleeding Room

The Bleeding Room turned out to be rather small, with a sink and glossy-topped benches. The benches were positioned around the walls, with the sink next to the door. In one corner there was a large metal cylinder with CO_2/Carbon Dioxide chalked on the side. A rubber tube led from the cylinder to a plastic bucket which had a loose-fitting lid. On the side was written 'Gas Chamber'.

On the wall was a medicine cabinet and on the door of the cabinet was a note that exclaimed *Key in office!* Glass fronted cupboards contained cotton wool and boxes of needles and syringes. Various sizes of bottles were positioned throughout the room. In one corner there was a set of weighing scales, a sterilisation kettle and a set of clippers designed for use on animal fur.

700 made a mental note of the questions he would ask 605 on his return to the quarantine area. The thought had occurred to him, of course, that he would not return to that particular room again unless he went down with an infection but he hoped that would not be the case. Anyway, he had more pressing situations to deal with at the moment. The questions could wait.

The man placed 700 on the bench, asked the girl to get a rubber mat and then leaned over to reach the fur clippers.

700 could not help but think it was about to receive a shampoo, set and blow dry.

To him it seemed as though the plot was definitely thickening. It was even becoming interesting. "What next?" he asked himself.

The large girl, her finger still bleeding beneath its hastily-applied dressing, returned with a rubber mat as requested.

"I hope you have disinfected that wound," said the man in the green jacket. "Shouldn't bother about any anti-tetanus treatment though if I were you. You'll probably be dead by the time the night's out!"

"Aye that's all right for you," she replied, laughing.

She had obviously got over the shock of being attacked by 700. Inwardly they all knew it was likely to happen once in a while. Provided that it did not become a regular habit, they would tolerate the fact that some rabbits occasionally reacted to staff invading their private domain. It was really a case of the rabbit exercising its territorial rights. All good, wild-animal stuff. It happens in the human world in the same manner anyway, and all humans know it.

"You can carry on now," said the man.

"So you want *The Terror* trimmed on each side?"

700 shook with both excitement and expectation. "What is all this for?" he wondered, unable to think of an explanation.

The girl picked up the trimmers, being careful to avoid 700's sharp end. She placed her left hand behind the rabbit's ears and commenced trimming the fur on the animal's right side.

"What a funny sensation this is," chuckled 700.

After a while he settled down and began to enjoy the feeling of the cutters going up and down his side. The steady hum from the electric motor was very soothing. He began to doze.

He had almost drifted off when a stinging sensation shot through his side. "Sorry old bun," said the girl apologetically. "Didn't mean to hurt you. Clippers slipped," she mumbled.

Silly fool, thought 700. *Bet she meant it!*

The girl continued trimming until the job was complete. 700 now felt rather chilly. After all, a portion of his nice warm coat of fur was now lying in a pile on the bench.

What a waste of effort in growing that lot, he thought. *Could have spent my time more usefully if I had known what was going to happen.*

The girl pushed the pile of fur off the bench in to a plastic bin which was strategically placed close to the bench. Some of the hairs lifted up in to the air and were caught in the draughts of air created by the air conditioning units. They rose like single fragments of cotton wool; higher and higher they went before disappearing against the background of the emulsioned walls and ceiling.

"Onward to heaven, the burrow in the sky!" smiled 700.

He began to sneeze in unison with the girl as the hairs began to penetrate their nostrils. She was able to use a handkerchief but poor old 700 had to put up with the discomfort.

Oh, to be human, he thought to himself.

The girl had carelessly left the trimmers running on the bench and now the vibration of the motor was causing them to slowly but steadily move towards the end of the bench. Suddenly, there was no bench left for them to travel across and the trimmers went crashing to the hard floor below.

"Blast!" shouted the girl. "I bet they'll be broken now."

The motor was still running, though the tone of the trimmers had changed. She picked them up from the floor, switched the motor off and on a few times and then tried them out on old 700. Three distinct grazes appeared behind the track of the clipper blade. Obviously, they would now be useless for the remainder of the rabbits.

At that moment, the man in the green jacket returned. The girl explained what had happened to the trimmers.

"Nell, you've had it now," he said. "That will come off your wages next week."

"Go on," she said. "They don't cost that much."

"Oh yes they do!" he joked. "Very, very expensive they are!"

She knew he was just kidding. The firm was so wealthy that they could be replaced, in solid gold, without them missing the expenditure.

"The only thing is that the remaining rabbits will have to be left until tomorrow," added the man in the green jacket.

"OK," she replied. "I will phone the lab boys to let them know. I suppose they will blame us for not having replacement clippers on site."

"Too true, duckie."

The girl went to phone the lab and a few moments later returned with a white-coated scientist, who was later followed by an assistant.

They all looked at the solitary bundle of fur sat on the bench.

"Looks more like a pound of mince," said the scientist, pointing at 700. The rabbit quite fancied testing his teeth again on this particular human.

Cheeky old sod, he thought to himself. *Who does he think he is?*

"Oh well," said the man in the white coat. "There isn't much point in hurrying if there is only one bun to inject."

"Let's all go to tea, in that case!" chimed the assistant, unenthusiastic about work but very enthusiastic at the thought of tea.

There was a general cheer of approval followed by a mad rush for the door. The sound of swishing starched coats and human footsteps quickly moved along the narrow corridor. There was a loud bang as the caffeine-starved mini mob erupted out of the building.

The cacophony also upset the pack of beagles which were also housed next door.

The weather had been so mild the beagles had been allowed to enter their outside enclosure. The noise of the dogs barking was terrifying to a rabbit, though the noise of fourteen beagles would terrify a lot of humans as well. The barking went on and on, upsetting everyone in the animal house.

700 was intrigued at the presence of such canine quadrupeds in an animal house.

He had never encountered such beasts before, although he had been warned by his friends and relatives never to trust

31

dogs. Oddly enough, he had been endowed with a natural distrust of them.

Something to do with self-preservation, he thought.

After a while, the animals began to get accustomed to the noise of the barking dogs. Above the incessant racket, 700 became aware of a strange scuffling noise nearby.

The door of the Bleeding Room had been left partly open. A white, whiskery nose appeared round the corner of the door.

"Is that a small rabbit?" wondered 700. "No, the nose is too sharp. It's got pink eyes, like me, although admittedly they're a lot smaller."

The white furry body came further in to view. It had a long and narrow body and a long, tapered tail about the length of a pencil. It was a large albino rat.

Chapter 6
The Albino Rat

The rat looked up at 700, stared for a while and then suddenly piped up. "Hello, bun. How's life?"

700 was still fascinated by the tail on the rat. So much so, in fact, that he did not actually catch the rat's question.

"Are you deaf, bun?" asked the rat.

"Oh, no, sorry. What was that?" cried 700.

"I asked how life was with you?" repeated the rat. "Rather noisy."

It was then that 700 noticed something even more odd about the rat. Under its belly he noticed a metal tube. It seemed very much out of place in such a position. He felt compelled to ask about the purpose of the tube.

"I say, Rat," shouted 700 above the noise of the beagles. "Excuse me asking but what is the tube for?"

"Oh that," replied Rat. "A good piece of surgery you might say. Very expertly done by a skilful scientist. It's called a cannula, I believe."

"What's a cannula?"

"It's the thing in my belly."

"Well yes, I know that," said 700, getting eager for an answer to his serious question.

"It is used to drain off fluid," said Rat.

"But why should you have fluid drained off? Were you born with a fault in your plumbing?"

"No, you silly ass!" laughed Rat. "I'm taking part in a necessary experiment. They give me drugs, then they open the cannula via a small valve and draw off some fluid, which they then test for some by-products. It helps them understand the way the drugs are processed by mammals. It's important stuff for improving medicinal treatment for animal and human health alike, you know."

"Oh, thank you. Very interesting," said 700.

"And slightly uncomfortable, too," added Rat.

"I can imagine. I wouldn't like it myself."

"No need for you to worry. They don't use rabbits for this series of experiments."

"Thank God," replied 700. "Long may that policy last!"

Rat continued his journey around the room, nosing in to every corner. "Rat," called 700. "Do you like it here?"

"Can be warm and comfortable, which is good, but sometimes wet and dangerous," replied Rat.

"What do you mean by wet and dangerous?"

"Well, take last weekend for example. Our room has an automatic watering system through which we are supplied our twenty-four-hour requirement of water. The water is fed to each cage through a pipe which has a valve on the end. Sometimes the valves forget to shut properly, or some silly rat chews the end off the tube. The water rushes out of the tube in to the cage and because the wire cage is itself positioned inside a plastic cage the water is unable to drain away. The plastic cage fills up with water and we have to swim to keep afloat. Unfortunately, the lid of the cage, which is made of metal wire, prevents anyone from jumping out so of course you can drown unless rescue comes in time."

Rat sat on his haunches to lick his forepaws before continuing. "Well, anyway, as I said, last weekend water leaked in to several cages and overflowed into the ones on the lower tier. You see, our cages are arranged in rows and tiers. A leakage in one tier will eventually leak down to the one below it and so on. Well, the water leaked and kept on leaking. Forty-seven of us drowned before staff arrived. I was damned lucky, I can tell you," said Rat with a tone of both relief and sadness. "I was sharing a cage with three others and I was the only survivor. I managed to nudge the lid towards one of the corners of the cage. I moved it just enough to be able to climb out. I looked around to find a safe place to hide and then later found a nice warm spot to dry off. I have been free ever since."

"You had better get out of here," said 700. "They will soon be back."

"Oh, I can look after myself. Don't worry."

Just then the outside door opened and footsteps were heard hurrying along the corridor. Rat had no time to get out of the room. The scientist's assistant appeared in the doorway.

700's heart sank at the thought of Rat's predicament. *How was he going to get out of this predicament?* wondered the rabbit.

At first the assistant did not notice Rat sitting in a corner of the room. Rat didn't move. He knew that any movement would betray his position, as after all he didn't have the camouflage of his wild counterparts. For once, he wished that he wasn't such a pure-bred creature. A little bit of mongrel would have been useful in this instance.

The assistant picked up some papers from the bench, blew off the accumulated dust and began to study the contents of the papers.

The main door was heard to open again and the remainder of the staff returned from their tea break. The assistant was distracted by the return of his colleagues and as a result he dropped one of the papers on the floor. He swore, bent down and picked up the offending sheet. Just then, the big girl stretched out her foot and playfully unbalanced the part-crouched assistant. He lost his balance and fell forward on to the dusty floor. He finished up looking straight at our friend, Rat.

It was difficult to decide who was more afraid.

The assistant rose from the floor like some new interplanetary missile. He forgot that his brain-box was still beneath the bench, and head and bench met with a great impact. The assistant once again found himself flat on the floor.

"Bloody Hell," he cried. "You silly cow! When are you going to grow up?"

Although everyone was embarrassed by the verbal savagery of the attack, they knew that it was only meant for one specific member of the team. Oh, yes. They were an observant bunch.

The girl burst in to tears. "You're crude and horrible," she mumbled. "I'm going to report you."

Poor old Rat just sat there waiting for his time to come. He knew that there was little chance of escape. However, he was like 700 in as much as he was quite capable of putting up a fight.

The assistant regained as much of his consciousness as he was accustomed to having. He remembered that somewhere in the commotion he had encountered a white rat.

"There is a bloody big rat under there!" he shouted.

"Go on, that's an angel," said the man in the green jacket.

"I may be semi-conscious but I'm not dead yet," said the assistant. "Bloody angel, indeed!"

They all went down to see the spectacle of a white angel. The ragging continued in the meantime.

"Look, can't someone catch that bloody thing before it runs off?" prompted the scientist.

The assistant didn't like rats but had suffered enough that day so he thought he would have a go in order to re-establish his position in the tribe.

Rat was ready for him. The assistant's hand gingerly came towards him. He stood on his hind legs, took up a boxing stance and then lunged at the ungloved fingers. After his parry, Rat returned to a defensive stance, still standing on his hind legs. He was a formidable opponent for any human while he was enraged and in this position.

"Holy Hell," uttered the assistant. "I've never seen a rat act like that before. I'm getting the hell out of here." And he most certainly did! The door slammed and he was gone. The others were not too brave now. Their laughter had stopped.

"Go on!" said the scientist to the girl. "Do your stuff," he said with both authority and some degree of fear.

The girl was known to have a way with horses. At this moment, everyone in the room hoped that nature had provided rat and horse with the similarities required for a peaceful, wound-free capture. Nobody was really confident of victory.

The girl waited patiently, (as all women do?) Rat began to ignore the stares, settled down on all fours and commenced to investigate the walls of the room. For one brief moment his back was turned towards the girl. She saw her chance and grabbed for the long, extended tail. Rat immediately began to claw at the floor in a vain attempt to escape. The floor was too slippery. He finished up running on the spot like some old donkey on a treadmill. The girl raised rat by the tail so that he was suspended in a most undignified manner two feet above the floor.

Rat now had to act fast. What trick of survival could he use apart from using his teeth? He attempted to turn his body upwards against gravity in order to catch his captive's fingers. It was no use. He was just going to use up vital energy. His instinct now took over in a final, desperate move. To the horror of the audience he began to spin his body and tail around the point of capture. Rat fell to the floor, leaving the outer skin of his tail firmly held by a shocked female. She immediately vomited on to the floor and fled out of the room.

The speed at which Rat had secured his release left him a little disorientated. He looked round at his 'new' tail, which was now a silvery white bony-looking thing.

Apart from the colour it was even more repulsive to a human than it had appeared in the undamaged state. The outer skin lay where it had landed after being discarded by the fleeing girl. It looked like the cast-off skin of some reptile, though not a very big reptile you understand. Just a little one.

"Why must rats have such revolting habits?" asked the girl as she returned to the battle scene. "They can look quite attractive with their nice white coats and little pink eyes, but they go and spoil it. I doubt if I will ever touch one again."

Not wishing to jeopardise man's attempts to study medicine, or her own career, she thought that she had better clarify her previous negative remark. "I'll be alright tomorrow." she exclaimed.

"Thank God for that," said the scientist, laughing.

The most experienced animal handler was the man in the green jacket. He donned a glove and very confidently moved towards Rat. He was quick to place his spread-out fingers over rat's back. Rat twisted round and bit once more, though this time the hand was not removed from the field of battle. His teeth had not gone deep enough to puncture the glove. Rat was as good as caught.

"Get me a rat cage!" cried the captor. A cage was duly brought through and rat was deposited inside.

"This experiment is finished now," said the man in the green jacket. "The flood at the weekend put an end to that. This rat is for the chop."

The assistant must have sensed that all was now safe and he returned to the Bleeding Room.

"Well, John Wayne," said the scientist sarcastically. "How's our hero?" The assistant remained silent.

"Place the rat in to the chamber," said the man in the green jacket.

The orders were duly carried out and the CO_2 was turned on. Rat gradually became drowsy as the gas sent him to sleep. He passed quietly away. The corpse was removed, the cannula extracted and rat was placed in a polythene bag ready for incineration.

700 just sat still. It had all been so quick that he could not believe that he had even witnessed the events. He dare not think about his own fate. Oh, to get back to the safety of his cage – or even freedom!

Chapter 7
700 Meets 605 Again

The scientist turned his attention to 700.

"What are we going to do with this bun?" asked the assistant.

"I intended to use a group for intradermal, multi-site," replied the scientist. "But because the trimmers are out of action we'll just have to wait."

"What do you mean by intradermal, multi-site?" asked the assistant.

"We will inject the substance under investigation in to the shaved areas just under the top layer of skin, that is to say, in to the dermal layers. We will inject very small quantities. It is a skilful procedure which does not seem to hurt the rabbit. They are not daft, you know. They soon let you know when you hurt them.

"You see, what I am after is a new test for a certain hormone. We want to be able to measure the presence of the hormone to aid diagnosis of health problems in animals and humans. The whole basis of the test depends on me obtaining rabbit antibodies to the hormone. By injecting the rabbit with the hormone, we should be able to induce a good antibody response. In some respects, this is akin to us being immunised against tuberculosis or some other foreign organism."

"I see," said the assistant, interested but a little lost.

"After a few weeks, we then bleed the rabbit from an ear vein; a painless procedure by any person's standards. We continue bleeding at various intervals thereafter until we have the desired quality and quantity of antibodies. The antibodies are present in the serum which is formed when a bottle of blood clots. The red blood cells stick together by a very complex process and the gold-coloured liquid which is squeezed out is in fact the serum. The test or assay which I am developing is used for many hormones and proteins and helps in the diagnosis of some forms of cancer, diabetes, pregnancy, spina bifida, dwarfism and thyroid conditions."

"It is a very useful and sensitive technique, then," said the assistant.

"Oh yes, there is no doubt about that. Nothing better at the moment."

"Animals are essential, then," acknowledged the assistant.

"We are very grateful for their contribution. One could sensibly argue that many rabbits in the world have done more for man than many humans have. It is distasteful that we have to use creatures who can do little to alter their fate in life but we all hope that one day other means will be found."

"I quite agree," nodded the assistant. "The use of animals is the worst aspect of our work. Take the incidents today, for example. The danger of being bitten, the trouble and cost of delays and then of course you have the cost of feeding and housing.

"That's right," agreed the scientist. "In addition, you also have the hazard of developing an allergy to the animal fur and skin scrapings."

"You mean like horse-dander allergies and things like that?" queried the assistant.

The scientist nodded in agreement.

The scientist returned to the job in hand and decided to put 700 back in to his cage until the next day. "Let's go back to the lab," he said.

At the door of the Quarantine Room the assistant reminded the scientist that 700 should not actually go back in to that room, given that there was a chance that he may have picked up an infection which would spread to the quarantined creatures.

It didn't make too much sense when you think about it, but that is the way animal houses are run.

700 was placed in a cage in another room. He was alone, surrounded by empty cages. There was only the background noise of the dogs barking and the regular drone from the air conditioning to keep him company.

The scientist and the other members of staff stood talking outside the room in which 700 was experiencing his quota of solitary confinement. They were discussing the rearrangement of the animals and the possibility of moving more rabbits in to 700's room. The scientist was insisting that all rabbits involved in his studies should be housed in the same room in order to avoid any needless searching. Eventually, the senior member of the animal house staff conceded and gave permission for none other than 605 to be moved out of quarantine. 700 was going to have company!

Chapter 8
Reasons Behind Operation Upset

605 duly arrived on the scene. "Hello again," she cried. "How's my old mate?"

"Much gladdened by your arrival," replied 700. "At least I will now have someone to talk to. There is a lot I want to ask you about life in this environment. I feel like I want to run away but I am too securely caged."

"Oh, don't get like that," said 605. "Your mood will pass and by tomorrow you will feel different."

"Don't mention tomorrow," groaned 700. "It's tomorrow that I am worried about."

"Tomorrow may never come," said 605 in her wisdom. "If it is any consolation, the more you worry today the less will happen tomorrow. So go on and worry, waste your time and energy. The most serious things in life happen without planning and are quite unexpected."

"Oh, I do hope you are right." 700 didn't sound convinced.

"Look, let's talk about things which can happen to others and not to ourselves. Take, for example, mice. They are so cheap and of such convenient size that they are used in experiments that would be unsuitable for rabbits. They are frequently used to test skin reactions to drugs, chemicals and cancer-producing agents. I must point out, though, that the animals concerned may also benefit from the knowledge gained. Any farmer, vet, cat or dog owner et cetera will tell you about the number of drugs which are available for animal health. Humans do not always escape being accidental guinea-pigs either, you know. Drugs have to be tried in humans at the final stage and there have been many instances of hazardous products being made available. The true effects of the human population have often been recognised only when it is too late. They can only get an indication of a drug's potential from the work on animals or live tissue cells.

"Some humans think quite strongly that animals should ever be used for such things as medical investigations but I must point out again that it will benefit us all in the end. There is no real answer to the problem other than responsible study with minimum numbers of animals. They could of course stop all progress in medicine. After all, man and animal have survived for generations with only natural selection to help.

The weak die and the healthy survive.

"Of course, it is difficult for man to accept such a simple way of life. He has an active brain and hands with which to carry out his thoughts. Other animals would be restricted by their inability to use tools and by their general inability to coordinate the necessary movements for such a complex life pattern. Quite simply, the world is open for humans to conquer and to destroy."

"I suppose it must be very difficult to accept the current state of things when you have the brain and ability to alter it," said 700.

"Yes, I can imagine that to be the case," agreed 605. "But I do feel that if an animal has such control over his environment he should know when to stop."

"That's quite right," said 700. "But look at the number of racing drivers, for example, that are killed because they participate in one race too many. At least, as I understand from the broadcasts I overhear."

"Quite correct! The art in survival is to know just when to move and to know when you have progressed far enough. Personally, I cannot think where humans are all going to go," continued 605. "They seem to breed so fast within fixed areas that they cause contamination of their environment, upset the temperature balance of the air with excess CO_2 and heat production, and above all release poisonous chemicals all over the place. If they could only see the contaminants in the air they breathe, they would surely be more careful.

"Like dirty water, you mean?" chimed in 700.

"That's correct," said 605. "It's very much a case of 'out of sight, out of mind' with them. They waste good land as if it were in plentiful supply. In fact, they generally live as if everything is going to be available forever. Of course, you could argue that our wild rabbit colleagues have the same attitude to life. They would breed all day if they had the chance."

700 laughed at the truth of 605's observations.

"Where do you get your information from?" asked 700.

"From the radio which is sometimes switched on by the animal house staff when they are going about their work, and from the arguments that they have on occasion. I wouldn't go so far as to say that they have discussions as such, because things tend to get heated very quickly. To define the racket as a discussion would be erroneous in the extreme!"

The emotional incident over the rat and the loss of its tail convinced 700 that 605 was quite right in her observation of their ability to argue. He was sure, however, that it was all light-hearted stuff.

"How do they bleed animals, other than our sort?" asked 700, changing the subject.

"Well," said 605. "The horses, donkeys and sheep are bled from the jugular vein in the neck. It is expertly done and doesn't hurt. A human would liken it to giving a pint of blood to the blood-transfusion people. The only difference being the quantity and lack of a cup of tea at the end of it."

700 and 605 laughed at the thought of a donkey sitting on a stool drinking tea. "Poor old mice have, in the past, got a bit of a raw deal," continued 605. "What do you mean?"

"Well, they are very small and it is not always to take off blood from them. They do have a nice convenient tail vein which is normally used, though."

"I suppose they benefit from the work that is done?" wondered 700.

"Yes, of course," replied 605. "They get sick and expect treatment just like us. It is nice to think, however, that most people really care about us. So long as they don't get too carried away with their beliefs, at least."

"Can you explain that last statement?" said 700.

"Well, they sometimes break into establishments and set fire to the buildings, let animals out and damage the property. You can imagine how bad it is for an animal which has had a protected life to be let loose in the wild. The temperature outside is often a lot lower than the temperature to which we grow accustomed to in here. The food is contaminated with germs that we have never encountered before and is, therefore, potentially dangerous.

"Some of us would have great difficulty readjusting to the harsh realities of having to fight and compete for food. Due to our colouring, you and I would both be very conspicuous in the wild. Predators would soon spot us and give chase. After sitting in a cage for such a long time I doubt if either of us could run very fast or far, so death would soon come."

"I know, I wouldn't be able to outrun very much," said 700, sadly. "What a way to go, not a nice death."

"Let's change the subject," said 605. "We are just getting morbid. Did you hear the joke about the two rabbits, one from Edinburgh and one from Cardiff?"

"No, I don't think so."

"Well then. What did the male Edinburgh rabbit say to the female Cardiff rabbit?"

"I can't think," said 700. "Probably something like *Och aye the noo, hoos yer sporran*."

"No, you twit! He said, *Hello Welsh rarebit, can I have a taffie apple!*"

"How corny can you get?" laughed 700. "I think I prefer you when you are serious. Look, the hours in the day are quite long for us. Let's further discuss the things you've said about humans and the way they live."

"OK," agreed 605. "Question some of the things that I have said."

"Let me think. There was one thing you said about them breeding too fast.

Surely it is a big world out there, isn't it?"

"Sure thing," nodded 605. "But they are not evenly spread throughout the world and the land mass is very much smaller than the water mass. When you get above a certain concentration of humans in one spot you see social pressures arising which would otherwise not exist. You end up with so much lack of freedom and so many different groups of people wanting to put something right that the conflict becomes everyone's problem. But there is no sense, to my way of thinking, in shooting off in to space with the intention of colonising some other planet.

"You see," continued 605 as she gathered her thoughts together. "These people have the ability and resources to build a utopia on Earth. Unfortunately, what is utopia for one may not be utopia for another. In other words, there would have to be several utopias constructed with all common desires provided on a shared basis. The population would have to be controlled so its density and the extreme lifestyles of each group would not affect the freedom of the people."

"Like noisy people and quiet people living too close together?" asked 700.

"A good, simple example! Like a bagpiper living next to a book-club fanatic." 700 beamed at the agreement from his learned friend.

"The problem is, 700, that a quiet person can live a quiet life without upsetting a noisy person but a noisy person will always upset a quiet person. They may have a lot in common and may share many things in life, this one essential point of disagreement can make life intolerable for the quiet-natured person."

"There must be room for them to live their own lifestyles without treading on each other's ear holes, as it were?"

"That's it in a nut shell. Or an ear defender!" said 605. "In many parts of man's world, they cannot help treading on each other's toes. Some of them even travel by plane over many miles to deliberately tread on another's toes. Silly idiots. Thank God we rabbits aren't so daft."

"Yes, there are advantages in being like us," nodded 700. "Eat, drink, eat some more, sleep and breed if you get the chance. If you breed too much you don't eat, and if you don't eat you feel hungry and don't sleep. So you search for more food, come to a river which blocks your path, you dive in and get too much water and so you drown."

605 laughed at 700's somewhat dubious deductions. "You are a pessimist!"

"Going back to this utopia bit," said 700. "Don't you agree that man has gone part of the way to building utopias?"

"Oh sure, but he keeps upsetting the balance of his civilisation. What you must do is carefully develop a system which is in balance and then make slight readjustments.

Man is so stupid that he upsets the balance by allowing those who want changes to take place and who want an important role in the community to take charge. Some are constructive psychopaths! Man is always trying to catch up on himself in the belief that change is progress, and progress is good. They have now reached the stage where progress in medicine is considered of doubtful value because the number of old people is a burden and the population in most countries is too high. They are working less and less and demanding more free time.

"In a few years from now they will have no countryside left in which to spend their free time. This is all right if you like pubs, bingo and indoor entertainment but what about the people who like an outdoor country life? There was a serious talk about rationing the numbers who can visit certain scenic beauty spots. How can man be so stupid as to get himself in to such a farcical situation? Life is absolutely intolerable already for many of them. Their cities are so congested that they cannot park their vehicles and the city fathers use intolerable tricks and schemes to discourage their fellow humans from using those vehicles.

"It appears to me that one half of the human population treats the other half as if they are some inferior breed of animal. Someone is always calling for legislation against something. You would think that after all this time that man would have his world better organised."

"Of course, the lack of perfect organisation is probably due to man's unsettled and discontented nature," said 700.

"That's just it," came the reply. "They don't know when to stop. They have the power to stop this so-called 'progress' but they would much rather allow everything go too far and then complain about the loss of the things held so dear when they were young."

"There is a lot of truth in that statement, that you do not miss that which you have never had," nodded 700.

"Soon they will not be content with flying to Spain for their holidays. They will want to fly to the Moon. Or further," prophesied 605.

"Overall, do you think they are happier than wild rabbits?" asked 700.

Sparrow

"No sir!" answered 605 in an instant. "I must admit, however, that when a human is ill it probably has a more comfortable time than a wild rabbit but there again, a human is more likely to get injured or sick because its way of life is so complex.

Furthermore, a lot of them are constitutionally weak because of their continued survival due to medical aid. A rabbit in the same condition would die and would not be able to pass on the weak genes.

"I've heard of some dreadful cases recently where hospital staff have gone on strike. The poor sick humans in the hospitals and those waiting entry are the ones who suffer. The very individuals in their society who are completely innocent and, in many cases, too ill to survive without treatment. It is my opinion that when a society stoops so low then they would be better returning to the wild."

"I quite agree, or they should bring out a law forbidding hospital staff from striking."

"That's it," said 605. "If you don't like the conditions then go elsewhere. If too many leave after a contract has run out at least the authorities would have prior knowledge of future staffing numbers. Conditions could then be adjusted to encourage recruitment. The advantage of this system is that no patient should have to be moved out of bed or hospital due to a lightning strike. The armed forces are organised on similar lines and as a result you end up with a true volunteer force which is more tolerant. The wrong type of person should be discouraged from joining the hospital service. By being stricter in this way it would encourage people to move in to the job which suits them better."

"Yes, they would have to be more careful in making a decision. Like humans getting married, the easier it is to divorce, the less important is the decision to get married." said 700.

"On the proverbial nail!" cried 605. "You what?"

"Let's help put them on the right track," said 605. "I don't follow."

"Look at it this way old bun."

"I'm younger than you, by the way," interrupted 700.

"Seriously now," continued 605. "I think humans in this country need a shake-up. They need to be made to think about what is going to happen if they continue the way they are going. I'm not saying that the older generation are at fault because they already realise that the world they are living in is in many ways not as good as it used to be. The younger generations are the ones that need a good shake."

"OK," agreed 700, "But won't it be difficult to shake up the young without upsetting the old?"

"Oh sure, but you must remember that those over forty have all experienced some form of military service or the years of World War Two. They have a different approach to life. I'm not saying it's all good but the younger ones seem to be taking too much for granted."

"In any case, we are dying at the hands of all age groups. We are at their mercy and therefore have nothing to lose by taking action."

"That's the spirit! Let's go out fighting!"

"There is just one problem," said 700. "How do we get out of here?"

"I have thought about exactly that many times," said 605. "It will be quite easy, really. We will muster 'The Grapevine' to help. Via this system of communication, we will be able to muster the aid of our wild colleagues and also those few humans with which we can converse."

"You mean that we can communicate with certain humans?" asked 700.

"Yes, it is a sort of telepathy which operates between a limit number of animals and people," said 605. "The nearest contact is an old engineer who lives near here. He has now retired but in his later years used to maintain the country lanes around here. I first heard of him through one of the sparrows who looks in on us."

"So you intend to muster his help to get us out?"

"That's it! We will then get accommodation and from there we will organise ourselves, and begin *Operation Upset*!"

Chapter 9
Sparrow

"When does Sparrow usually visit?" wondered 700.

"Oh, any time," said 605. "It depends on the time of year and the supply of food.

If food is plentiful around the local fields, he pops by every half an hour or so. In fact, look! I think that's him up on the roof right now."

"Oh hell, I can't see out of the window," cried 700 with disappointment. "Never mind, he will fly down as soon as he sees me. He is probably expecting me to be over in the Quarantine Room.

"I can see his shadow on the wall!" said 700 excitedly.

"That's not much good to us," laughed 605. "Wait, look! Here he comes now.

He's landing on the window ledge. Hi there, Sparrow! Full of good seed, I hope?"

"Yes," said Sparrow. "It's been a good day today. Land of plenty! Got a bit of a tummy ache, though. Some stupid farmer's been spraying with weed killer. I think he got to the grain that I had for my breakfast. Last week I drank water which was contaminated with diesel oil. River water isn't much better these days. It only needs a thin film of oil to cover the surface for us to end up with a mouthful. If it's not that, it's fertiliser and plastics which wash in to the ponds and streams. They should be more careful, you know. I flew over a duck just now that had been caught in a fishing line that some human had left tied to a log. He may be lucky this time, at least. I was able to contact *Grapevine* and arrange for help to be sent. Perhaps Old George the road-man will cut him loose."

"I'm sure he will," said 605. "But that reminds me, we were just discussing what I've spoken about with you before many times."

"I bet it was about sorting out the humans!" smiled Sparrow. "That's it. Look mate, I wanted to get out of here quick. I then want accommodation which will be suitable for a battle HQ." 605's voice was steady and firm as she spoke.

"Why have you made up your mind to do this now?" asked Sparrow.

"Well, I have a friend here who thinks in similar terms and who is going to die at the pleasure of these humans in the same way that I will. Suddenly, everything seems right to be taking action."

"I remember that one time you had ideas of giving a name to your plan," said the little bird.

"*Operation Upset. O-P-E-R-A-T-I-O-N U-P-S-E-T,*" repeated 605, spelling it out. "And by the way, meet my friend number 700. You can't see him because his cage is in the wrong place."

Sparrow laughed and chirped, "Hi bun!" to the invisible 700.

"Hi Sparrow!" came the shouted reply. "Pleased to have you around and glad to think you are going to help with Op. Upset."

"Sure thing!" said Sparrow. "Wouldn't miss this for the world. Takes the boredom out of life. But look, I must go. It may take some time to contact everyone."

"OK, goodbye and good luck!" shouted the rabbits in unison. With a dull flutter, Sparrow disappeared.

Sparrow sped up and over the roof tops and across the open fields. The fields were larger now than they had been because the farmers had removed so many of the dividing hedges. It was a warm, sunny day and apart from the nagging pain in his stomach he was really enjoying it! All days were not the same for Sparrow and his like. The weather dominated his whole existence but man didn't help that much, either, when he came to think about it. Admittedly, man grew a lot of grain and that obviously helped Sparrow with his food supply but man was using too many chemicals these days.

Every week was becoming more and more difficult for Sparrow to survive. Even the towns did not provide him with much comfort. There was a shortage of nice big gardens and warm chimney pots. Everything seemed to be covered in cement or cold flagstones. The human vandals were destroying the new trees in the estates and many houses only had grass patches, at most. Everyone seemed to be applying pesticides and spraying against one thing or the other and the next thing, without knowing what it was all really about.

Oh, for the old days, thought Sparrow.

He thought about the stories handed down from his parents and grandparents and all those before. How the estates had had large vegetable gardens with nice fresh fruit. The birds acted as the insecticides in those days and in addition deposited a helpful layer of manure on the crops. Earthworms did the digging and aerating of the lawns and the moles chased the earthworms, further helping churn the garden over in the process – albeit often in the wrong place. Too much digging and too many molehills meant the moles inadvertently helped create jobs. And fur for gloves.

Berries were not contaminated with oil and mud sprayed up from roads back then. Leaves of trees remained light green for much longer than they do now. The elm trees towered upwards, looking healthy and strong as they broke up what may otherwise have been a flat landscape. Even the winter snow was whiter and remained that colour for longer than it does now. You could eat snow to quench a thirst, even if too much hurt your stomach, whereas now it was dirty and contaminated with airborne debris and chemicals.

Sometimes Sparrow could see towards the industrial midlands where that specific area could easily be identified by the haze of filth and fumes rising in a long blanket up to a height of at least two thousand feet. Sparrow had never flown at that height himself but he had heard from many a transient pigeon that to fly through such a cloud was both unpleasant and exhausting. In fact, some pigeons reckoned that it was worth the effort to fly up and over the haze even though it meant reaching such a great height.

Old George

Wagtail

Sparrow sighed at the loss and began to chase a butterfly to take his mind off the pain in his stomach. He had found in the past that violent aerobatics sometimes helped to move a pain but of course this time the pain was due to poison rather than a physical obstruction. The butterfly was like a tissue paper, first in front of him and then to the left and then the right. It appeared to be able to turn on the spot. To chase a butterfly was a very exacting art. Good practice for the development of coordination in young birds.

The butterflies were rarely caught when pursued by a single bird. It really demanded team work to guarantee success. Of course, the reward always went to the bird which made the final grasp. There was never enough for the supporting team. In fact, they used up more energy in catching the butterfly than they recovered from digesting the catch.

To eat seeds on the ground was far more economical.

Forgetting the butterfly, Sparrow's pain became worse as he cleared the last brick wall before descending in to Old George's garden. He landed on the lawn outside the little thatched cottage. He did not have sufficient energy to fly the other seven or eight feet to the window ledge. Now that his journey was over, he had more time to think about the pain.

He felt really bad.

Chapter 10
Wagtail and Old George

A pied-wagtail landed on the grass beside Sparrow and, not sensing that anything was wrong, he twittered, "Nice day, Sparrow!"

Sparrow groaned and collapsed on the grass.

Wagtail came running across, the way that wagtails do. His tail bobbed up and down incessantly, helping him to keep his balance. "Oh gosh, oh dear!" he panicked to himself. "I don't like emergencies! I never know what to do. Perhaps if I fed him a dead fly, he might recover?"

Wagtail was a fly-catching expert, especially when it came to catching the flies that hovered above a lawn. *No,* he thought. *The best thing to do is to get Old George.*

Unknown to Wagtail at that moment, Old George was already heading to the rescue. He had sensed that something was wrong in his garden. He opened the door and saw Wagtail flapping about, clearly in a bit of a stew.

"Quick, George! Over here! Sparrow has collapsed. He seems to be very ill indeed."

"Now then, now then," cried Old George. "Don't get your bowels in an uproar.

It may not be too serious."

Inwardly, Old George was not happy at the sight of Sparrow lying there. He had seen too much of this in recent times. In fact, it was happening all the time now. Almost every day he saw a creature suffering. What was happening to his beautiful country? What was man doing to the place, the animals and birds, to his plants and to himself? Man was becoming his own cancer. Spreading slowly but surely in to every corner of the world, destroying most of the things that had always held true and replacing them with (dis)organised chaos.

Old George walked slowly towards Sparrow, then bent down and picked him up.

Sparrow lay motionless, his heart rate had slowed to a dangerous level.

"Oh dear, oh dear. You are in a bad way," said George. "But never mind, we'll see what can be done!"

Wagtail flew up and down with excitement. At last, Sparrow was going to be saved! He knew that without question, as his confidence in Old George was unquestionable.

"Coming inside to see how we gets along?" asked George to Wagtail.

"Oh yes, please," replied Wagtail. "I'm very concerned about him. He seems very ill to me."

"Come along then old spud," said George in his friendly way.

The trio went in to the house and Old George placed Sparrow on the draining board. He then filled a rubber hot-water bottle from the copper kettle that sat atop the stove, wrapped Sparrow in a handkerchief and placed him carefully on the warm bottle. Next, he lifted down a very old bottle of smelling salts from a shelf and held the open neck close to Sparrow's beak. Sparrow suddenly gave a squeak and his body visibly expanded as he took a great involuntary gulp of air. His little body shook with the shock of inhaling such a horrible vapour.

"There we are, now," said George. "Don't worry, you are going to be alright!

Try to sit up and tell me what is wrong."

In a very quiet and weak voice Sparrow told Old George about the pain. He was just about to go on to discuss the other reason for his visit when Old George butted in.

"That's enough chatter for now," said George. "We'll look at the problem of your health first. We can leave the rest until later."

Old George went to a cupboard and took a small green coloured bottle from a shelf. Although a small bottle, it looked terribly important with its hexagonal shape and vertical ribs on five sides. The contents had obviously run down the sides of the bottle because there was a thin film of brown running from the cork to the base. George began to shake the contents of the mysterious bottle and even more of the contents spilled out.

Sparrow sat there, wondering if there would be anything left in the bottle by the time George had finished. The contents began to run down George's hand.

"Oh dear, I've sprung a leak!" cried Old George. "What a waste, what a waste!"

Wagtail smiled to himself. Old George was beginning to fail, but then, he was now eighty-five years old.

"Now then, me old Sparrow," said George. "It ain't much, but it's very potent." Sparrow did as he was told, having every faith in George's wisdom.

"There now, that should do. Take a rest for an hour or two," advised Old George, "Then tell me all about your reason for coming in this direction."

Sparrow was very fortunate in being a bird, in some respects, because although they tend to be very sensitive to poisons, they can also recover very fast indeed.

Something to do with their relatively high metabolic rate, it was thought.

Sparrow soon felt a lot better and began to walk about the draining board on which he had been placed.

"Come on, old son," said George. "Let's go in to the front room and you can tell me about everything."

"Well," said Sparrow in a still-weak voice. "I've been asked to come here to get your help in releasing some rabbits from the research place. They feel that they could do more good, in some respects, if they had their freedom. They feel, like you and I, that the world is being abused by man and that his way of life needs to be redirected."

"That's very true," agreed Old George. "No damn respect for anyone. Too many youngsters have no respect for an old man like myself, and it goes a lot deeper than that."

Sparrow nodded. "My rabbit friends, Number 700 and Number 605, want to organise an animal protest. Their idea, I think, is to show man how vulnerable he really is in his comfortable world. Man thinks that he is all superior and that he can do what the hell he likes, as and when he pleases."

"I'm with you all the way," agreed Old George, nodding. "I don't suppose I'll be around much longer anyway, so I might as well try to help a worthy cause. I used to be very content with my life but somehow everything has changed since the old days.

"Back when I was younger and working on the maintenance of the country lanes, people would stop to exchange the time of day. Most used to walk two or three miles to the village to do their shopping. They didn't rush around. They did that shopping on one day of the week, one day to do a big wash of their clothes and linen. At harvest time everybody mucked in to help. The fields and lanes were full of activity until the job was done.

"It made a lot of work for me, of course, because I had to clean up the extra straw that had blown off the carts on to my road. Had to keep them clean in those days or the squire would complain! Didn't mind, though. That was my job and I took great pride in it! It was a pleasure to work outside in the fresh air. Never felt tired in those days, not like how I did just before I retired. I was older of course, but somehow the air had developed an oily sort of smell. Not very strong if you understand but it was certainly there. I could detect it. It was there all right. Now that I'm retired, I don't come into contact with roads very much, so the air in my lungs is a little less full of fumes than it was at least.

"I used to get really annoyed with the many drivers who tore about the lanes as if they hadn't a minute to live. Some of them didn't, of course, but they weren't aware of it. Saw three people killed in my time, within seconds of passing me. What a waste, a sad waste. Where were they going to? They were trying to save time and make rapid progress for the sake of it. They succeeded in getting to the grave ahead of schedule and in fact held up the progress of their own employer by leaving a job unfinished. All their training and knowledge went with them. They left the material things for which they had worked and saved for. Their knowledge is probably useless where they are now but that's a question to which we have no answer."

Sparrow and Wagtail had listened to every word Old George had said and found themselves agreeing to it. He was a wise old man indeed.

Chapter 11
A Tragedy in George's Life

"I was really sickened by some of those city humans," continued Old George. "When they injured my old Gert. She was a good soul. Married sixty years we were! No family in all of those years but we were very happy. We liked a quiet life in the countryside with the trees, sky and animals for company. We used to help where and when we could, as I still do now. On a Friday night I used to finish early, go home and get tea and then the pair of us would toddle off down to the village hall. One night, we left at the usual ten o'clock and started to walk home. Gert suddenly remembered that she hadn't paid old Mrs Smith for the week's milk so I dashed off back inside.

"I settled our dues and jogged my way back home as quickly as I could. I saw the paraffin lamp burning in the window as usual. We often used those old styles of lamps to remind us of old times that were fond memories for us both. It felt more homely like, a gentle yellow glow that seemed to relax the mind. I think that fierce bright light and noise tends to stimulate a person too much. That's what's wrong with these young 'uns today. That and drugs or alcohol and they go damned daft! I know it only affects a percentage of them but a small percentage today means a hell of a lot of youngsters, and when you get them moving about the country the way they do, they can be a real menace!

"Now where was I," said Old George, composing himself. "Oh yes, I was telling you about my Old Gert and the paraffin lamp. Well, as I said, the lamp was lit and the glow was hitting the garden path a treat it were. Really homely to a chap comin' home at night. Well, I was so busy watching my old feet going up the path that I didn't see the front door half open. I got quite a shock, see, when it moved before I got anywhere near the latch.

"Most unlike me Gert, I remember thinking to meself. Getting careless in her old age. Could let too many mice in, I thought. Well, I goes in and all was quiet like, except for a low moan from behind the big settee. It were then that I noticed that the old vase on the mantelpiece had been removed and was lying on the floor. Next to the vase was a shoe and then I saw old Gert. She was lying face down with blood streaming from a head wound. I didn't know what to do for a minute. Cor, it were real deep and bad like.

"I was worried sick. I turned her on her back and she was able to tell me that two young men had rushed in after she had lit the lamp. They demanded money and pushed her about. Well, I ask you, what was the sense in attacking an old road-man's wife? We didn't have any spare cash, except the rent money. Well, they beat her about so she told them to take the contents of the vase and they did just that, then hit her over the 'ead wi' it. Eeh, she were bad.

"We didn't have a phone so I had to get up to the big house to phone the police. They got the ambulance but it were too late. She passed away shortly after. They caught the young villains shortly after that. At the court, one of the thugs said that he needed the money to give him a start in life. He reckoned that the old lady hadn't needed the money! What an attitude to life, I tell you. Do you know, I read that in Scotland a few years ago one in five seventeen-year-olds was convicted of a crime? There were 200 attempted murders, too!"

It was obvious that Old George still felt ill at the thought of his Gert in those last lonely hours. How their quiet life had come to such an abrupt end, much in the way that many animals die at the hands of man. It was such a cruel world. No wonder Old George was willing to help 700 and 605 in their campaign.

Like many animals he felt that the world was unreal and that they didn't really belong there any more. They felt out of place with their views on life.

Chapter 12
Get Ready to Escape

Old George turned to Sparrow and asked about the plan to release the imprisoned 700 and 605. Sparrow was now feeling a great deal better and his wings were getting stronger every minute.

"Well," said Sparrow, "I think time is short. 700 may be injected tomorrow so we need to plan the escape for tonight."

"That's fine wi' me," replied George. "As soon as darkness falls, I'll get cracking."

"There is one problem," said Wagtail. "They have a security guard and an Alsatian. Unless we get word to the Alsatian in advance, he may attack you."

"You leave that to me," piped up Sparrow. "I'll have a word with owl about that.

He does a lot of night shift and I am sure he has already made friends with the Alsatian."

"Good," said Old George. "Although I have a way with animals, I cannot expect the Alsatian to be kind to a stranger intruding in his territory!"

"Right then!" exclaimed an increasingly-strong Sparrow. "I'll leave you to get the rabbits out and perhaps you could carry them to your home for further discussion? After all, nothing has really been organised yet."

"OK," agreed Old George. "We will form a war committee in my little cottage!

Sparrow and Wagtail stayed for tea with Old George and then flew off together.

Wagtail had agreed to accompany Sparrow in case he had a relapse. Old George had given Sparrow a tiny piece of straw that he had impregnated with the wonder medicine – in case of emergencies. It was unlikely, therefore, that Sparrow would suffer any more but Wagtail thought that he would still accompany Sparrow. He also had to admit that he was now rather eager to help in *Operation Upset.*

The feathered pair soon arrived back at the animal house window, where they beckoned to 605. She looked up and saw that Sparrow had returned with a friend.

"Meet Wagtail!" shouted Sparrow. "He is going to help!"

"Hi, Wagtail," said 605. "Welcome to the team!"

"Hello, and cheerio!" said Wagtail. "Excuse me leaving but I don't much like sitting on window sills. Much prefer walking on grass! Sparrow will relay the plans and discussions to me."

"Oh, hang on, Wagtail. There isn't much to relay at the moment!" reminded Sparrow. "Remember, we've just come back to tell 605 and 700 to be ready for Old George's arrival tonight."

"Tonight?!" shouted the excited rabbits. "Yippee!" they roared. "Tonight, tonight!" they exclaimed.

700 ran seven times around the inside of his cage. He promised himself that tonight, on his release, he would run seven times around the outside of his cage.

"OK," said Sparrow. "I can see that you have heard what I said. We must go now because we are both very hungry. Us birds use up energy so fast that we must feed almost constantly!"

"Bye for now, then!" shouted the rabbits. "And thanks a million. That's the best news anyone has ever brought me." said the buns in unison.

"Great minds think alike." said 700. "Agreed!"

The animal house was now quiet. The staff began to wash up and prepare for home. The atmosphere was electric in the room which contained the two potential escapees. The outside door was locked behind the last member of staff that left. The animals were now alone once more.

605 began to worry about the other animals in the house. "What will we do about the other occupants when we are about to escape?" she asked.

"I was just thinking about that myself," said 700.

"A bit of a problem really," mused 605. "I know that some of the guinea pigs have not been used in experiments and are leading the Life of Reilly."

"Who is this Reilly?" asked 700.

"Oh, he was an Irish rabbit who accidentally tunnelled in to a distillery," said 605 with a smile.

"I see," said 700. He wasn't really sure he had been given a truthful reply. "Anyway, these guinea pigs may prefer to stay," continued 605. "In which case, I think we will adopt a general policy of helping those who want to escape, and to leave those who prefer to stay. After all, it would be against our aims to enforce things upon those we are hoping to help. Only certain members of the human race will be dictated to and animals will be free to live their own lives."

"Sounds fine to me, then," said 700. "We will await the arrival of Old George. I only hope that Sparrow will manage to get the support of Owl, or else that Alsatian could be the ruination of the plan!"

"Have no fear, Owl will help. Sparrow is well-liked around these parts. He could get a cat to like a dog!"

Chapter 13
The Escape

Once they had seen Owl, Wagtail and Sparrow each had a good fill before darkness fell. They then made their way to Old George's cottage. It was like the blind leading the blind, neither of them being much accustomed to night navigation.

"I can't see a damn thing at this speed!" cried Sparrow in a tone of panic. "Well, we can't slow down or we'll lose all lift and come crashing to the ground," replied Wagtail. "If we go higher, we'll be safer but we won't be able to see the cottage."

"Of course, we will!" said Sparrow optimistically. "Let's climb up."

The two aerial terrorists soared to above tree height and levelled out. Eventually they began to relax. Down below they could see the occasional landmark. It was not as difficult as they had feared and soon they saw a familiar field, one they knew was close to Old George's place. They began their descent and were almost on the ground when Wagtail suddenly heard a resounding crash and a cry for help. He quickly dropped to the ground and looked back over the airspace through which he had just flown. He couldn't see a thing but again he heard a cry for help.

He flew back in the general direction of the noise and spotted something fluttering in a large net which had been placed over some fruit bushes. Sure enough, there was Sparrow with legs where his feet should have been and wings all tangled-up in netting.

"Get me out of here," shouted Sparrow. "The blood is rushing to my head and my beak hurts! I went straight in to a pole!"

Wagtail flew up to where Sparrow was so entangled and began to release his luckless friend.

"Oh, my beak, my beak," sobbed Sparrow. "God, it does hurt!"

Wagtail flew down to pick up an old piece of rag which was lying on the ground. Between them, they managed to combine their nest-building skills to weave the strands of the rag around Sparrow's beak. He did look a poor sight.

"Never mind," said Wagtail. "I suppose we will have a lot of war wounds before we are finished. Let's walk to the cottage from here. Or rather, you hop and I'll walk!" The little bird laughed.

"It's alright for you," muttered Sparrow. "Walk, indeed! If you were a proper bird you would hop like me."

The pair of grounded astronauts eventually arrived at the cottage. Old George had to laugh at the sight of their first casualty. He did look ill!

"Come away in," said George. "I'm just about to get ready."

Old George got out his darkest clothes so that he would be difficult to spot in the dark. He covered his white beard in soot from the chimney and covered his collarless neck with an old scarf, donned an old jacket and boots, clicked his heels in military fashion and declared that he was ready.

By this time, Sparrow was so excited that he had not noticed the absence of pain in his beak. It was obvious that this adventure and many more to come were going to make a big difference to them all.

Old George moved towards the door, at the same time inviting the two birds to jump in to his top pocket. The old jacket was of such an age that the pocket was stretched out of all proportion. There was enough room in that pocket for a couple of crows, let alone two of the smaller varieties of bird!

Sparrow and Wagtail settled in and made themselves comfortable. They were going to enjoy this particular journey – or so they thought!

They soon found that Old George's swaying gait was not the most conducive to either sleep or rest. Apart from the left-hand side of the jacket flying open and closing it also went up and down in a predictable, ceaseless rhythm each time George put his left foot on the ground. Sparrow soon felt unwell again, and Wagtail didn't feel too good either! It became clear that a complaint would have to be lodged with the wearer of the jacket.

Owl

"Stop, I've had enough," shouted Sparrow. "I feel sick!"

"So do I," agreed Wagtail. "Let me get out!"

"There now," said George. "Feeling sea sick, I suppose? Oh dear, oh dear. I suppose the movement is a lot different to flying! Oh, I am sorry! You'd better go back to the cottage. Wait under the thatch for me, I won't be too long. Unless I'm caught!"

Wagtail and Sparrow soon forgot the importance of the mission. Getting on to firm ground had become much more attractive to them! They flew out of George's pocket and said goodbye to the old man.

"See you soon," remarked Old George.

George soon arrived at the animal house after detouring around the security guard's office. Sparrow had arranged for Owl to keep a look out for Old George and on seeing the man arrive, Owl descended from a tree which overlooked the future site of action.

"Hello George!"

"Oh, hello Owl," replied Old George. "Can you tell me what you know about the security guard's routine?"

"Yes," said Owl. "He will soon be round with his dog. I understand from Sparrow that you would like me to have a quiet word with Alsatian?"

"Yes please," said George. "We don't want any mishaps tonight!" Owl nodded. "You go in to hiding until I give the all clear."

"Right," agreed George before dashing off to a nearby place of refuge.

Owl took up watch on a nearby fence and waited patiently for the appearance of dog and guard. Within a short time, the tell-tale heavy breathing of a dog on a lead reached Owl's ears. Alsatian appeared first, followed by the guard. The dog was pulling on the lead like mad.

The guard suddenly stopped outside the animal house and checked the security of that part of the building. He placed a looped end of the dog's lead over a hook in the wall and disappeared behind a large bin for a pee.

Owl saw his chance to have a word with Alsatian. "Psst! Psst!"

Alsatian looked over towards Owl. He could just about see the creature in the darkness.

"Psst! Psst!" Owl was doing his best to get the brute's attention but the dog looked mystified. "Psst, you silly bugger!"

At last Alsatian got the message. He signalled for Owl to approach and the bird glided silently over.

"You are a dim bugger," cried Owl. "Why didn't you pay attention to me?"

"I'm sorry," said Alsatian. "I thought you were imitating my boss passing water."

"Oh my God," replied Owl. "Now I've heard everything! No wonder the Germans use your type for herding sheep. That's all you are fit for!"

"No need to be offensive," answered Alsatian grumpily. "What do you want, anyway?"

"I don't have time to explain properly. Just ignore any noises you hear tonight and pretend not to see a certain old man who will be appearing."

"But why?" asked Alsatian. "I'll get pensioned off if I don't do my job!"

"If you do your job too well tonight, I'll pension you off myself," said Owl. "I'll pick you up and drop you from that elm tree over there, see!"

"OK, OK, OK," said the dog. "I've seen what you can do to mice."

"Aye, well don't forget it," smiled Owl. "I'll explain everything at a later date."

Owl had been watching the guard out of the corner of his eye. He began to turn around, ready to walk back towards Alsatian. Owl took off and flew in to the darkness without a sound.

"Oh hell, what was that?" exclaimed the guard out loud as he sensed motion. "Bloody place is haunted! Must have been a bat or something. Come on, dog. Let's get the hell out of here. Too eerie for me!"

The dog and the nervous guard disappeared into the gloom and, once they were safely out of sight, Owl flew across to Old George to tell him that everything was ready.

George nodded, took up a metal bar that he had found and made his way to the animal house door. With one wrench of the metal bar the wood beside the lock split in to pieces. The initial entry had been easy!

George walked briskly in to the animal house and could just about see by means of the dim security lights. He went in to each room, opening cages as he went. He soon came to 700 and 605.

"I'm George," he smiled. "Glad to see you!"

"We are more than glad to see you," said 700.

"Look," began George. "Get the animals organised in to those who want to help the cause and those who would prefer to stay. Time is short. Forget the dogs, they will cause too many complications for us. It's a pity but they will have to stay."

"Right," said 605. "I'll see to that."

605 bounced off to organise the excited masses of fur. At the final count they had the support of forty rabbits, twenty guinea pigs and one hundred mice.

"Muster outside," shouted Old George. "All fall in!"

The motley army 'fell in' as it were and then began the trek back to Old George's place. As they passed the security office, Alsatian looked up in amazement. The smiling human winked at Alsatian – and Alsatian winked back, albeit with a puzzled expression on his face.

Chapter 14
Planning the First Attack

At the cottage gate, Old George decided to billet his army in the garden shed. He invited the ringleaders, 700 and 605, in to his house – they had a lot to organise. For one thing, they had to form a warfare committee. George told the rabbits to make themselves comfortable beside the fire. Seeing it was late, he stoked up the fire with the intention of letting it burn all night in case the rabbits should get cold. All three made themselves comfortable and the discussions began.

"How many should we have on the committee?" asked Old George.

"Just the three of us, with additional advisers if required later," said 605.

"Agreed," nodded 700 and George.

"Less trouble with arguments that way," added 700. "All agreed then," smiled George. "Three it is!"

"When do we start?" asked 700.

"Tomorrow," replied Old George immediately. "Agreed," nodded the two rabbits.

"What a good committee this is," laughed 700. "We will never argue! Now, who is going to be the first victim of *Operation Upset*?"

"It doesn't really matter," said Old George. "We will have to start somewhere."

"Well," said 605. "You have suffered most, George, by the hands of muggers.

Let's start with them!"

"Couldn't agree more," said George. "It will be a great honour to start with them! The only thing is, we must affect the whole country at once! We must make assault and mugging a dangerous pastime for the villain."

He thought for a while, stroking his beard before picking up his old clay pipe.

The soot which he had applied to his beard came off in his hand. "Oh dear, oh dear," he cried. "I had forgotten about my make-up!"

700 and 605 laughed at the old man's predicament. George wiped his dirty hand on his trousers, lit his pipe from a lighted taper and settled back to think. After a few moments of silence, he looked up. "This is going to require a lot of reliable help from the animal kingdom," said George, looking hopefully at the two rabbits.

"What about us?" said a weak voice from outside. "What was that?" wondered 605.

700 looked towards the window and saw the figures of Sparrow and Wagtail. "Oh my gosh," cried Old George. "I had forgotten about them!"

George got up from his chair and opened the door. In wandered the two feathered colleagues.

"Couldn't get in," said Sparrow. "Had to hide in the garden because there's netting on the thatch!"

"Oh, I am sorry," said Old George. "Too much excitement tonight. My old mind just ain't accustomed to it! Anyway, we are all here now, so come in and make yourselves at home."

The old man settled himself back by the fire before speaking again. "Look, I think we will need the help of Sparrow and Wagtail – and Owl, too – on more than an occasional basis. I think they should be allowed to sit in on our *Operation Upset* discussions. They will be of great benefit to all of us as messengers."

"Agreed!" said 605 and 700 in unison. "I'm sure they will not cause us any trouble," added the latter. "I'm sure they will be indispensable!"

"Right then," said Old George. "Tomorrow we will have to inform Owl of our decision. I am sure he will be delighted to help us. Now let's get back to our arrangements for attacking those villainous mugger-types!"

"Look," piped up 605. "I have been thinking about this. It would appear to me that two general localities are involved. One is the quiet countryside area where muggers use the rural location to commit their deeds and the other is in the cities. To attack muggers in the countryside we will require the services of nocturnal country animals. To attack the city-muggers we will have to rely on the services of animals both day and night. Obviously, there will be exceptional attacks which we may miss but by and large we should make a devastating impact if we can cover both of the situations mentioned."

Everyone agreed, their minds racing as they became quite excited at the prospects. 700 smiled, "Boy, is this going to be great fun!"

Sparrow did a victory roll around the room and finished up, not entirely intentionally, in a vase of flowers. The others couldn't hide their laughter!

"You are a liability," laughed Wagtail. Sparrow picked himself up and quietly hopped in to a warm corner to dry off.

"Now then," said George. "It's clear we'll have to recruit owls, foxes and badgers for the countryside surveillance. Starlings, sparrows, dogs and cats are the most numerous and thus best choices for the towns. No mugger will suspect anything even if they see those animals moving around."

"Great, great," grinned 605. "What a great plan! Nobody would suspect that a fox or sparrow had any intention of attacking someone."

"Yippee," shouted 700. "I like this business! What a change in my life. I really feel that we are going to contribute such a lot to the world at large."

"Right," continued George before everyone got carried away. "Sparrow, you contact Owl and get the owls organised. Wagtail, get in touch with a fox and a badger so they can pass the message on to their kind. Oh, and get Alsatian to start passing the message on to all of the other dogs. And the cats! I'm sure some dogs have friendly relationships with their feline counterparts."

George relaxed for a moment before piping up again. "Oh! Just remembered.

Sparrow, you contact the sparrows and starlings, too!"

"Crikey," said Sparrow. "Just leave everything to me! I've got enough to do!"

"Oh, go on," said Old George with a warm tone. "It will only take a minute of your time."

"Yes, I suppose so," replied Sparrow with a cheeky grin. "I was only kidding. It will be great fun, really."

"OK then," said George. "That is that for tonight. Now, a good rest before our first attack under *Operation Upset*."

Chapter 15
Muggers

The next morning and after an early breakfast, the little messengers went on their errands. Old George fed the remainder of the escapees with what scraps he had. The guinea pigs were a bit of a problem. Old George wasn't quite sure where they would fit in to *Operation Upset* but he knew they had been determined to try and help. He decided to have a word with the lead guinea pig, who was currently out in the garden shed.

"How do you feel about helping to sort out the humans? You have probably heard by now that we are going to prove to the country that humans are not the super-dominant race that they think they are."

The leader of the guinea pigs looked up at George. "Yes, we had heard mumblings to that effect."

"I'm concerned about whether you'll be able to help properly." said George, honestly.

"Well, we can gnaw at things," said the leader. "Quite well, in fact. Just let us run around and we will also find food for ourselves, and others if we can. Don't worry about us."

Old George was pleased that the leader had agreed to look for food. It would save him a lot of time and worry! It was agreed that the guinea pigs would be called upon for gnawing jobs, perhaps supporting the mice and rats in that kind of operation as well.

George returned to the cottage and awaited the return of Wagtail and Sparrow.

700 and 605 were quite restless with excitement. It was a long wait.

Eventually, the two birds returned and were quite full of themselves! They had achieved their objectives without a hitch. Apparently, the badgers were only too pleased to get their own back on man because he had built a road across one of their runs and many badgers had been killed attempting to cross it. The foxes were annoyed with the local hunts who had bred them just to be released for chasing. For generations man had dominated the fox but now it was small wonder that the fox might look to attack mankind's domesticated animals in order to get their own back.

Many animals looked down at the foxes for this sort of behaviour but most could at least partly understand their reasoning.

"What about the sparrows and starlings?" asked George.

"In full support, both," said Sparrow. "They feel, however, that all men should suffer. I did point out that man does supply a lot of food and heat to many of us, so it really is only rogues that should be sought out!"

"That's good," said George. "I don't want to be attacked!"

"No, no. You will be all right," confirmed Sparrow. "They agreed with my sentiment and are all behind us now. As far as we're concerned, *Operation Upset* can go in to operation right away! In fact, the city animals are already on the lookout now. The muggers had better be looking out, too. Especially when darkness falls!"

"Just marvellous," smiled Old George. "I think we will now await the arrival of the morning papers. I am sure that there will be some unusual happenings reported.

"Better still," said Sparrow. "What about the radio?"

"Oh my! Of course!" laughed George. "How stupid of me! The local station should report something soon after it happens, though mugging isn't too common in these parts."

"No, but mysterious circumstances befalling muggers is of interest to any reporter," said 605.

"You are right there," smiled 700.

"OK, we will put the radio on all day just to see what happens," said George as he wandered over to the radio and switched if on. He was no fan of pop music so wasn't entirely happy to oblige.

The same was not true of Wagtail, who was soon bouncing up and down in time with the music.

"A regular Fred Astaire!" chuckled Sparrow.

"Travolta, you mean," said 605. "You've got to move with the times, you know."

"Who is this Travolta?" asked Old George.

"Oh, he's a new dance idol," replied Wagtail. "He was in a musical called Grease."

"Look, even old Wagtail knows who he is," said 700. "A regular little encyclopaedia," snapped Sparrow.

Wagtail stuck his tongue out at his friend. "Thruuuuuppp!" he said with a rude gasp.

Old George smiled to himself. It was all good-natured fun. His house was happier now, far happier than it had been since Gert had been taken from him.

Lunch time came and went but still there was no announcement of unusual animal behaviour. Old George began to think that mugging might have gone out of fashion and that there'd been nothing for the animals to stop. Everyone began to feel dejected.

"It's early days yet," said George, detecting the mood. "Any minute now something is bound to happen. Some foolish human will attack someone."

It was now just minutes before 2pm.

"The news will soon be on," continued George after a pause. "Let's sit around and wait for the announcements. Quick, Sparrow, get the mice and guinea pigs in to have a listen."

Just then, Owl arrived – looking half awake.

"Come in," said George. "You are probably just in time to hear something of interest. The news is about to come on."

It was thirty seconds before 2pm. The room filled up with all manner of interested parties; a motley crew of one man, two rabbits, three birds, twenty guinea pigs – along with one hundred mice and a further forty rabbits outside. Four of the rabbits had their noses pressed hard against the window pane.

They did look funny! The mice tried to climb up on to the ledge of the window sill but without success, scampering towards the door and squeezing through a gap there instead. Old George ended up with a century of mice spread over his shoulders and the arm of the chair.

His little living-room looked like a zoo.

The radio chimed 2pm and the announcer wished his unseen audience *good afternoon.*

"Good afternoon!" shouted one hundred mice. Everyone in the room laughed with nervous excitement. "This is the two o'clock news."

There was a deathly silence. 700 sneezed. Owl flapped his wings. "Oh, do shut up!" shouted one of the fawn-coloured guinea pigs.

"The prime minister has today decided to visit President Amin of Uganda. The purpose of his visit is to investigate the president's claim that he is the prime minister's grandfather."

"Oh, that'll cause a flap," said 605.

"My God, you are right there," agreed 700.

The newscaster continued on various political themes, each as boring as the last. "…and now, an interesting case of crime prevention," boomed the voice on the radio, himself sounding perked up by the article. "It has been reported that a man was dragged out of hiding by two cats and a dog following a mugging in the city this morning. Passers-by stated that they had never before seen such an astonishing sight, claiming that the cats had been sitting on a wall close to an area which is notorious for muggings.

"While the area had only seen a handful of muggings in the recent months," continued the reporter, "It bore the hallmarks of an emerging trend and the police were beginning to take notice. An eye-witness said that the mugger struck an old lady of about eighty and made off with her purse. The cats immediately followed, soon joined by a dog in the ensuing chase.

"The mugger attempted to hide but was grabbed by the animals, who began to savage and maul the thief. The villain eventually managed to escape, albeit streaming with blood.

The purse was returned to the old lady by the dog. All three animals sped off and disappeared. The same eye-witness said it appeared as if the animals had been working together, as though they had been coordinated and trained for the job."

"Yippee!" shouted 605, as the other animals cheered along with enthusiasm. "What a great first success," said 700 with a broad smile.

The radio announcer continued on with the sports news. Old George got up with tears in his eyes.

"Unbelievable, absolutely unbelievable," he muttered through his tears.

Everyone in the ensemble began to cry with excitement and surprised. None of them could have hoped for a more successful start to *Operation Upset*.

Old George switched off the radio and went to one of his cupboards. He removed a bottle of elderberry wine, shook off what must have been years of dust and poured out over a hundred tiny portions of drink into any container that he could find. Together, everyone toasted to *Operation Upset*.

By nine o'clock that evening the anti-mugging episodes had increased to such a strange level that MPs were beginning to take note, with remarks being made about the situation prior to the close of session in the House of Commons. Observers who had witnessed animal attacks or running men obviously thought that there were too many savage animals going about. Not all were yet aware that the men on the run had all been villains, as all too often the actual mugging took place out of sight of any witnesses.

The animals, however, saw everything.

They were unable to attack before the offence took place but they were uniformly quick to attack once they were sure a crime had taken place.

Some muggers were so stupid that they attempted to continue with their foul operations. The cats in particular had good memories so started to follow known muggers. In one case, twenty cats followed a known mugger for three hours until he finally sought refuge in a hospital. He was so stricken with fear that he was immediately admitted to a psychiatric ward.

Fox (in his younger days)

George was now more than satisfied with the day's events. He knew, however, that the real test of skill would come after dark. He felt that the best was yet to come! The household went to rest, quite content to await the daily papers and the following day's news bulletins.

Midnight struck on the old clock of the sideboard. Old George woke up and looked over towards the bedroom window. He hadn't drawn the curtains and the moon was shining brightly. He could hear an owl screeching in the distance. *It wasn't as eerie a noise as it was when close by,* thought George to himself. *Quite a nice country noise, really.*

Suddenly, he heard a distinct change in the call and a moment later heard a fox screaming like a woman in agony. Now *that* was an eerie noise to anyone not accustomed to life in the countryside. George thought that there was an unusual amount of commotion from that one area and got out of his bed to look out the window. He could see a fire burning in the distance.

"That's strange," he said to himself. "The only thing over there is the road-making company's machines and their night-watchman's hut. Oh dear, is everything alright?"

Old George kept staring in the general direction of the fire and felt sure he could see a lot of large birds flying up and down. Occasionally he thought he could hear humans shouting. Suddenly, there was a large swooshing noise outside of his window. A pair of big eyes stared at Old George and a voice cried, "Open up! We need help!"

It was Owl. Old George opened the window and the bird flew on to his arm. "What's up?" asked the man. "In trouble?" For a moment, in his half-sleepy state, George had forgotten about Owl's commitment to *Operation Upset*.

"Trouble isn't close," said Owl. "We need reinforcements. A gang of humans have attacked the watch-keeper over at the roadworks. They attempted to steal his money but we managed to intervene. They, however, managed to set his hut alight. There are five of them but only two owls and a fox. The fox was kicked in the side and is badly hurt, while my friend has a broken talon. He is still fighting on as we speak."

"Right," said George with urgency. "605, get all the rabbits together. Quickly!" Within minutes 605 had rounded up all of the rabbits in to an emergency army.

"Let's go," said George, who had managed to get his boots and coat on. "605, you run ahead with the others and direct the attack. Owl will guide you in."

The forty-two strong rabbit task-force bounded off behind owl, who flew steadily and very low over the fields. As they got closer to the fracas, they could see that the villains were winning the fight. Owl and 605 pitched in to the affray with the support of 700 and forty other sets of teeth. The villains let out yells of shock and pain as teeth sank in to their legs and arms. The owls attacked their necks and faces in vicious revenge. At last, one collapsed and two others fled in terror. The final two attempted to fight on by standing on top of a piece of machinery but the owls and rabbits had little trouble in throwing them off balance, toppling them to the ground where they were immediately pounced upon by the majority of the creatures. They soon lost consciousness, and no wonder.

Their wounds were as deep as they were severe.

605 mustered the army for a roll-call. By this time, George had arrived. He joined in the count and assessed the damage.

"Ten cut ears, one broken leg and two dead," said George, quietly.

605 looked over towards Fox. He was lying very still and looked as though he had broken ribs. The rabbit hopped over for a closer look. The fox didn't seem to be breathing.

"George," cried 605, worried. "Come over here and take a look at Fox. I think he is dead."

"Like hell I am," said a faint voice. "Just get my painful ribs bandaged up."

Old George took off his jacket and shirt, tore the cotton fabric of the latter up and began to bandage Fox's ribs. Up until now distracted by the casualties of the army, 700 suddenly remembered the most important victim of the villain's attack. Where was the watchman who must be lying injured somewhere?

Owl must have read 700's mind. "He's over here," shouted Owl. "He has come round but looks sickly. He is too old to have put up with such an attack. I'm glad the villains have taken the punishment that they have!"

"Quite so," said 700 as he hopped over towards where the old boy was sitting.

Old George joined the rabbit and bent down to speak to the watchman.

"Good Lord," said George with surprise. "If it ain't old Harry Prangle. You all right, 'arry?"

"Yes. Yes, I suppose so," said 'arry. "I'm not entirely sure what happened. It'll be tomorrow when it tells on me, I 'spose."

"Your old hut is burned to ashes," said 700. "Where are you going to go tonight?"

"I'll go to a lodging house," said 'arry. "I don't have a real home as such. All my folks are long since gone. Been orphaned since the war."

"Look," said George. "You could stay with us but I am sure the police will be along any minute. I'm sure a night in hospital would be the best thing for you right now."

"Ye', I does feel a bit queer-like, George," said 'arry. "I'd best do that. Get checked out."

Owl heard the wailing of a police siren in the distance. "Look out," he shouted. "The police are on the way. I can see a flashing blue light, though it's still a few miles out."

"Right, we're off," George said as he took to his feet. "Bye for now, 'arry, but come around when you're out of the hospital if you're stuck for anything."

"I'll do that," said Harry. "Thanks kindly. Oh, by the way George. What happened tonight? Where have all the animals come from? I've been dazed for ages."

"I'll tell you about it sometime," smiled George. "But for now, I must dash. Bye now."

"Bye," said 700.

"Cheery-bye," said Fox, cringing as the pain in his side got worse.

"Oh God, I suppose I'll 'ave to carry you," said George. He picked up Fox and staggered off in to the night, followed by his battle-weary army.

Chapter 16
Harry and the Police

The police car arrived on a quiet scene, though the sight of a pile of burning debris, a stunned-looking old man and three badly-bitten unconscious villains betrayed a more complicated tale.

"Good God," said the police sergeant as he stepped out of his vehicle. "What the hell has happened here?" He went over towards Old Harry to check on him.

"Been attacked. Three of the villains are lying over there," said Harry, pointing towards the motionless masses.

"You OK, old man?" asked the constable who had arrived with the sergeant. "Not too bad, I think. Been hit about the head a bit. I think I had better go to the hospital," replied Harry.

"Aye, OK," said the constable. "We'll have a look at the other three first."

The policeman walked slowly across to the bodies and gave each a gentle nudge.

Two responded with a groan, the third just lay there motionless.

"Let's try to bring them round," said the sergeant. Together with his constable, the sergeant gently slapped and shook the men. Two eventually came around but the third was still very ill. The sergeant radioed for an ambulance.

"What the hell's happened here tonight?" wondered the constable.

"Bit of a mystery to me," answered the sergeant. "Let's ask the old boy. These others aren't fit to run anywhere.

"What's your name?"

"Just call me 'arry."

"OK 'arry, now what went on here tonight?"

Harry was just about to say when he remembered about Old George's interest in the matter. He didn't want the police going to Old George's in case his old friend didn't want them to know about his involvement. Harry was in a spot. He didn't like the idea of not helping the police but what could he do? He had been in a dazed state for most of the incident so he didn't know the truth anyway.

"Well," he said after a pause. "I don't rightly know. These blokes, five of them, attacked me and tried to steal my money."

"What was your money kept in?" asked the sergeant. "A yellow tin."

The sergeant produced a dirty old tin which was more brown in colour than yellow, though it was obvious it had once been much brighter in cleaner times.

"This it? How much is inside?"

"Three hundred," said Harry with a sigh of relief.

The sergeant opened the tin and began counting the money. "Five, ten, fifteen…" He went on and on, "Two hundred," he gathered his breath. "Two hundred and five…" Eventually he reached the final note. "Three hundred and two pounds!"

"I'm better off than I thought," said Harry. "That's a good end to the night."

"Now what about these injuries?" said the constable. "These villains have got some queer-looking marks. Looks to me as though they've been savaged by an animal of some sort."

"You may be right," replied Harry. "You may just be right about that."

The two policemen were clearly dissatisfied with Harry's vague cooperation.

Both felt that there was a lot more to this business!

Just then, the ambulance could be heard approaching.

"Look, old boy," said the sergeant. "We will question you at the hospital, along with the villains. We must get to the bottom of this lot."

Harry knew that the villains would give the details of the story to the police, which would save him splitting on Old George. After all, his old friend and his army had done society a service tonight!

On arrival at the hospital the injured parties were cleaned up and put in to beds.

The police questioned the villains first and got some bizarre accounts of rabbits and foxes attacking them. When owls got mentioned as part of the story the police thought that the villains were either suffering from shock or were feeling the effect of drugs. The medical staff assured the police that the men were perfectly healthy and should have no problems telling the truth, but the police couldn't help but conclude that the villains were lying.

A senior CID chap was brought in to question the villains, their story interested him because of the weird cases he'd heard about on the radio. Was it true, he wondered, that animals were actually attacking villains? The detective decided to question Harry a bit more closely.

The old man admitted that the villains were telling the truth, but he did not divulge information about Old George. The police had to conclude that the animals had indeed been involved and that the incident was strikingly similar to others reported throughout the country. It was clear there was going to have to be some top-level discussions about these incidents. Something funny was going on!

A few days passed before Harry was allowed out. The firm he had worked for had bought him a new caravan to live in, small but luxurious. He was now better off than before!

Meanwhile, back at the cottage, Old George had been keeping busy nursing his casualties. He was kept very busy indeed. The group had decided to lay low for a while because George feared humans might panic at the thought of an animal uprising and begin a mass extermination programme. Old George was no fool, he knew that politicians drunk on power were quite likely to react in such ways and experience had taught him that the villain often received more consideration than the victim. Although it was obvious to the observer that the animal kingdom was attacking the criminal element, he was not convinced that he would get government support.

This is why he had to be secretive. Eventually, Man would get the message.

Chapter 17
And Now for the Vandals

The events so far had caused a minor panic throughout the country. The newspapers were full of statements and suggested explanations. Reporters were really jumping on the bandwagon! 700 and 605 had even heard reports that could not possibly have been true, including that animals were being blamed for attacks on innocent people! George was saddened by this turn of events and decided to call a meeting of his war cabinet.

Old George, 700, 605, Owl, Wagtail and Sparrow sat around the table to discuss the situation and determine their next course of action. 700 brought up the matter of the erroneous and misleading reports. He agreed that some pets would always attack their owners but unfortunately these events were casting a shadow on *Operation Upset*. It was quite obvious that the black sheep among the pet world would have to behave or risk ruining the whole thing. An ultimatum would have to go out to all animals in the country.

Aggression against Man would only be permitted after discussing the matter with the war cabinet of *Operation Upset*, unless it was in direct response to crimes being committed.

"And what's more," added 605 calmly, "If they do endanger *Operation Upset* in this way, we will have to exterminate them!"

"Oh dear," remarked Old George instantly. "I don't like the sound of that."

"Look at it this way," explained 605. "If we don't make it obvious that we are only interested in re-educating the unruly and irresponsible humans then the politicians will surely call in the armed forces to exterminate us. *We* will have gained nothing and *they* will have gained nothing. We will all lose."

"Quite right," shouted Owl. "I think we must continue, making it obvious that we are only after the villains in their society."

"Unfortunately, some scientists will have to be taught a lesson as well, and the humans may argue that they are innocent people," said George.

"I'm sure we can find a way round that problem," said Sparrow.

"Yes, I 'spose so," replied Old George.

"So we go on, do we?"

"Yes, yes!" cried everyone. "We go on!"

"So who is next on the list?" asked 700.

"I think we should continue with the muggers until mugging is stopped completely," offered 605.

"I agree," said George. "But in addition, I think we should take the war to the vandals as well."

"Yippee!" chirped Sparrow. "They damaged my nest three times last year. Little sods!"

"Aye, and they do worse than that," said George. "Much worse. An old friend of mine was an engine driver and he lost his eyesight through young idiots throwing stones at his train. The windscreen broke and the glass went everywhere. Terrible shame, it was. He had been an artist in his spare time and a damned good one, too! Lovely paintings of trains and the countryside he used to do. Even had one or two exhibitions in the village hall."

Wagtail cried at the thought of the train driver. It was a sad tale. To think that the quality and course of a person's life can be altered by one immature child. The child enjoys himself and goes home to forget it. The victim lives on for probably forty years or more without his eyesight.

"Aye, it makes you wonder whether people should have to go through some sort of selection or aptitude test before being allowed to reproduce! The most important thing a person does in life is to bring a child in to the world and yet there are neither requirements nor qualifications. Seems silly to me," said Wagtail.

"Well, never mind. We have the power to put some of these things right," said 700.

"Owl!" shouted George. "Set the word about that muggers and vandals are to be attacked. Furthermore, put out the warning to all pets and animals that they must only attack humans when acting under instruction from us as part of *Operation Upset*."

"Okey dokey," said Owl. "Will do! I only hope they obey."

"So do I," agreed 700. "Otherwise we'll all be for the high jump."

The party didn't have to wait long for reports of attacks against vandals to be reported. It appeared that the majority of destructive deeds were done by younger adults not much over the age of eighteen. Old George had always doubted the wisdom of generally lowering the age of adulthood from twenty-one to eighteen. He was the first to admit that physically the young people of the day were mature and healthy by psychologically many seemed to lack maturity. It was as if the brain hadn't caught up with the brawn. In fact, he got the impression that a young person with a good level of basic intelligence became more intelligent with sound feeding, because after all it was feeding rather evolution that had caused recent changes in the young and that inherent idiots and social misfits became more so on a similar diet. It was as if in the latter case bad genes and cells were developing in an enhanced way. It made sense to Old George. After all, why should diet only aid the development of brain cells and chemical reactions that lead to ideal social behaviour and not be able to cause enhancement of the cells and reactions that lead to unsocial behaviour?

Television, too, is the cause of a lot of trouble. It brought ideas and scenes in to the home which would otherwise have never been encountered. The behaviour and actions in cities like London were spreading out in to the country almost overnight, whereas in the old days it took years for ideas and ways of life to filter out. When watching television in colour the scenes are so realistic that one's reaction to violence and bloodshed is eventually dulled until the appearance of violence has no deterrent effect. Gaping wounds and death become commonplace every evening in the home, a place which should be a refuge from such things. The low morals of the script writers and the low morals of their characters are reflected in the televised product and in their writings. One is led to believe that this is the way everyone lives. It is all false to those who are wise to life but the young can only judge from what they see and unfortunately many parents set a bad example. They want to be single and yet married, without responsibility. Oh, what a mess!

It is often argued that cowboy films are just as bad for the young. Admittedly there is a lot of violence in such films but it is in a different country in a different era. It is not really possible to relate to the scenes. After leaving the cinema the viewer was soon brought back to reality by the traffic and the tarmac, by concrete and brick buildings. It was a different world, with not a horse or cow in sight (prostitutes excluded).

"What are you thinking about?" asked 700, looking at the old man. "Oh, er, nothing much," said Old George, stroking his beard. "Just day dreaming."

"Here is the news!" boomed the voice on the radio in the cottage. "It's the news, it's the news!" shouted Sparrow.

"Oh my, time flies," said George, getting comfy in his chair.

"Further attacks by animals on humans have been reported in Liverpool," began the announcer. "The attacks now seem to include vandals, with over twenty casualties reported in the past twenty-four hours. The wounds were so severe in some cases that lives may be threatened. The chief of police has called an emergency meeting to look at the details, which now appear to be taking on a set pattern.

"It would appear that there is little doubt that the cats and dogs in the area are definitely paying undue attention to wrongdoers. It has not yet been explained how the animals can tell one human from another, and they seem to know who to watch and who to ignore. In many instances other animals such as birds have been witnessed getting involved in the attacks.

"A spokesman for the Royal Veterinary College has concluded that a degree of intelligence and coordination of effort is being shown by the animals in a way which has never been seen before. He can only suggest that they have been specially bred and trained for the purpose, or that a new drug has been developed and released. The suggestion of the animals having been purpose-bred is countered by the fact the animals have only recently suddenly shown such a high level of cooperation and team work, while a drug consumed in a diet common to all animals must be dismissed as being the cause. It has already been found that numerous sources of food have been used by the animals involved in the coordinated attacks.

"The most horrific case was reported from a village churchyard where cats and rats from a nearby farm were aided by around thirty pigeons and sixty bats in attacking a gang of young hoodlums who had arrived on motorbikes. The motorcyclists had entered the churchyard and drove over the graves repeatedly before getting off their bikes and breaking up a number of gravestones. Several stone coffins were broken in to, with remains scattered around the church grounds. The animals intervened with such fervour that only one member of the gang managed to escape. He was left so terrified that he went to the nearest house in the village and entered without permission.

"Numerous rats gave chase and kept him housebound until the police arrived, having been called by an eyewitness. The old couple in the house that the youngster had entered were left unharmed by the rats. By the time the police arrived the churchyard was full of skeletons. There was not even a trace of the motorcyclists' clothing. While the motorcycles were undamaged, the bones had been licked dry and there was no sign of flesh or blood. A police spokesman said they had never seen anything like it."

Old George jumped up from his chair and hurriedly switched the radio off. "Oh dear, oh dear," he cried. "What have they done? I never wanted anything like that to happen! We must stop this before it gets any worse. Dear, dear, dear! Oh my God. Oh my God!"

Old George paced the room. The animals started to wail and cry. Nobody knew what to say! It was such a shock. They felt as though they had started a giant machine and suddenly didn't know how to control it. Everything was going wrong and getting out of control. George was heartbroken. He wished he had never started the whole thing.

"What a way to spend the rest of your life with this act on your conscience," he said. "Dear, dear, dear."

Somebody had to say something to console Old George. The animals all looked at each other.

"There now," said 605. "The animals in that episode got a bit too enthusiastic but maybe they knew more than us. Perhaps those youths on their motorcycles were really mean, really bad. Real outcasts. They sound pretty horrible to me."

"And me," chimed in 700. "And me, too," agreed Sparrow.

"Yeah, they deserve it," said Owl. "Should have been strung up."

"Oh now, let's not get like them," said Old George. "Let's not get too harsh."

"Look," said 605. "I'm going to find out more about the past history of those motorcyclists. I reckon they must have been really bad and the animal leader that night must have known who he was dealing with. Owl! Nip across to the farm next to the churchyard and see if you can find out anything which will help us to understand just why the animals attacked in such a severe way."

"Be right back," said Owl.

Owl flew off towards the desecrated graveyard and soon made contact with the local owl. He asked about the battle in the yard and was told to see *Big Puss,* the local dominant male farm cat.

Chapter 18
Big Puss

Big Puss

Big Puss turned out to be a massive black tom cat with a white splodge of fur on his nose. His coat glistened in the evening light. He was a magnificent moggy, obviously someone who got the best of everything.

Owl flew down to the bale of straw on which the cat was seated. "Well, what do you want?" asked Big Puss calmly.

Owl was usually very confident but Big Puss seemed to inhibit him in a strange sort of way.

"Oh, I erm, just want to enquire about the battle," said Owl. "The battle? What battle?" replied Big Puss in curious fashion.

"Oh, well, erm, the battle in the churchyard. When the motorcyclists were devoured by your army of supporters," answered Owl.

"I don't know what you're talking about," said Big Puss. "There was no battle around here."

The big cat started to lick his paws and wash his whiskers in the way that cats do. He looked up and beckoned to a scraggy Manx cat.

"Get me a mouse to eat!" he bellowed. "And make sure it's still warm. I don't like cold mice."

"Certainly, sir. As soon as possible," said the scraggy cat.

"Not soon, now!" boomed Big Puss. "You stupid, tail-less wonder. Can't even grow a bloody tail. Get me a mouse *now* or else I'll have *you* instead."

Neither the Manx cat nor Owl doubted the fact that Big Puss would have a piece of warm Manx in place of a bit of mouse. Though magnificent, he looked hungry and angry enough to eat anything.

Owl continued to question Big Puss about the battle. The big cat said nothing but then suddenly let fly at Owl, lashing out at him with his great claws. Owl just managed to jump in to the air and out of the way. One of his talons caught Big Puss on the nose and made it bleed. The cat was now even more angry than before, lunging again and again at Owl. The bird flew up on to a beam above Big Puss's head; the cat leapt upwards but fell short of his target by a few inches. The attack was too close for Owl and he flew up to a higher ledge on the gable end of the building.

"Frightened, eh?" asked Big Puss.

"No, just wiser than you," said Owl. "And a better flyer."

"Cheeky blighter," said Big Puss. "I'll set my army against you."

"No you won't," replied Owl. "You won't, because I could be useful to you for catching mice."

By chance, out of the corner of his eye Owl saw a mouse running across the floor of the building. He swooped down and with little trouble caught the creature. Owl flew back to the ledge.

Big Puss couldn't help but be impressed with Owl's efficiency.

"Very good, very good. I like the way you handle yourself. A very efficient mover."

"Now look," said Owl to the big moggy. "When you are old you will have to rely on birds like me to catch your food, so why not stay friends and stop attacking me?"

"Give me the mouse."

"Not until we come to an agreement," replied Owl.

"Okay, okay. You have a point. I like your courage. Nobody dares to make bargains with me."

Just then, a very tired, weary looking tail-less moggy came staggering round the corner. It was our friend, Manx.

"Where the hell have you been?" sneered Big Puss in a raised voice. "Where is my mouse? I want my mouse! Produce the mouse, or else!"

"I'm sorry," said Manx, weakly. "I couldn't find one."

"Jesus wept!" exclaimed Big Puss. "Can't find a mouse in this filthy hole of a farm yard? You must be blind!"

Big Puss sprang at the other cat and knocked him off his feet. Manx fled as quickly as he could.

"Give me that bloody mouse, you over-sized chicken!" shouted Big Puss to Owl. "Don't you address me in that way," said Owl. "I'm in charge of this situation. "I'm sorry, but I am hungry. Let me have that mouse."

Owl dropped the mouse on to the straw that was strewn across the floor. It immediately ran for cover but Big Puss charged after it and caught it easily. The mouse bit the cat's tongue and found itself released suddenly. It scurried away under a big piece of machinery. He was caught again, but again he bit deep in to Big Puss's tongue. The big cat threw the mouse in to the air but didn't manage to catch it again in its paws, instead knocking it on to the seat of a tractor. The mouse, by now quite dizzy, managed to run beneath the cab in to a gap that Big Puss could not squeeze in to in pursuit. The cat was defeated.

"Damn, damn, damn!" grumbled Big Puss. "I'll get that swine, don't you worry.

I'll get him, even if it's next week."

"Or next year. Or next year." added Owl.

Big Puss was too annoyed and out of breath to argue. Suddenly, his attitude towards Owl changed.

"About the battle. What do you nosey lot want to know?"

Owl was surprised at the cat's change of heart but thought that he'd best take the opportunity now, lest the animal change his mind again.

"Why so vicious an attack?" asked Owl. "Was it necessary to devour them?

What did you know about them?"

"They were a bad lot. A bad lot indeed," said Big Puss. "And anyway, I am in charge. I can do what I like."

Owl thought that he had better humour the cat. "Oh yes, of course. Quite right. You are very much in charge of this area."

"That gang had been in and out of prison for ages. Mugging, arson, vandalism, extortion. Animal cruelty. You name it, they've done it. Call it fate, if you like, that they came in to my patch. Made a big mistake, they did. I heard about *Operation Upset* and agreed with the idea of it, but I think you lot are too pussy-footed, as it were. Need to have more action to send the message home. That's what I say."

"Oh, sure," said Owl. "But you know that the humans will react badly to such savagery, don't you?"

"I owe nothing to humans. Couldn't care less, so long as I get fed."

"Okay, sure, but they could wipe you out for your actions. You must see sense or we could all be doomed."

"Shove off," said Big Puss. "I do things my way."

Owl tried to continue the conversation but could not reason with the cat. He saw no sense in staying any longer and, without saying goodbye, he took off and flew back to the cottage.

Old George was very sad when Owl told him of the lack of understanding shown by Big Puss. It was obvious that they would have to curb the severity of the cat's attacks but what could they do? He was a very strong opponent, and one that ruled over a large area.

605 sat next to think of a plan. Surely one cat could be controlled?

"Let's all sit and think on this," said 605. "We need a *think-tank* on this one. It is very important we come to the right decision."

"It appears to me," said Old George, "That we are now trying to show animals the folly of their own ways, instead of humans."

"Yes, but Big Puss is an exception," said 700. "We will soon pass that phase and get back to the proper line of attack. Let us say that we have been temporarily diverted from our main course."

"We could capture him," offered Sparrow, hopefully.

"Yes," said 700," But I think a lot of animals would get hurt in the process. It would need to be a commando type of attack, special forces," said Wagtail.

"Something like our rescue from the animal house," said 700.

"Oh, what a frustrating problem," said Old George. "As if we didn't have enough to worry about."

Just then there was a bang at the door. It had been struck so firmly it seemed as though the door almost collapsed!

"Good Lord!" exclaimed Old George. "What on Earth caused that?"

"Didn't sound like a proper knock to me," said Sparrow.

Again, the door rattled on its hinges from the impact of a second blow. This blow was followed up by a frenzied shout.

"Let me in, quick! Let me in!"

"Who on Earth is that?" asked 605, ears upright. "Quick, open the door!" shouted Owl.

Old George got up and with a mixture of swiftness and trepidation, opened the door.

A black shadow shot through the gap and into the room before darting beneath the sideboard.

"Good grief, what was that?" asked 700 in wide-eyed astonishment.

Owl had by far the best eyesight and had no difficulty in identifying the blur that dashed through the room. "It's only Big Puss," he said proudly.

"Oh my," said George. "I don't want trouble here. Tell him to go away! Fancy frightening me like that."

"Shut the door and don't tell a soul," said a voice from under the sideboard. "Don't let them catch me!"

The animals looked at each other, wondering what had reduced the terror of the farm to a nervous wreck.

"There now, you are safe here, provided you don't go all funny-like," said Old George, reluctantly picking up a poker in case of any trouble.

"I'll come out, I'll come out," said the feline voice. "But don't let anyone from outside see me."

"Okay, okay. Now come on out, sit on the arm of my chair and tell me all about it." Big Puss cautiously crawled out from his hiding place and after a quick look around, jumped on to the arm of the chair.

Old George lit his pipe and waited for the explanation for Big Puss's visit. The cat looked all out of joint and was still breathing heavily from the efforts of his frantic journey to the cottage.

"They've killed all the cats in the yard! They've spread poison everywhere!" he gasped. "It is carnage. Bodies of rats and birds are everywhere. Carnage! They fired shotguns at everything that moved."

"Now just a minute," cried Old George as he began putting two and two together. "Are you saying that men arrived at the farm and began to kill the animals? The animals who were involved in the battle against the motorcyclists?"

"Yes, yes! I was lucky to get away. Manx is dead, he ran in front of me to divert a gunman's attention. He was struck by the shot from a double-barrelled gun! To think I mocked him!"

Owl gasped at the thought of Manx dying to save Big Puss. *What a strange world,* he thought to himself. *Manx deserved better than that!*

"Who were the men?" asked 700.

"A mixture of pest control officers and police," said Big Puss. "They seemed to be very well organised. I suppose public opinion forced them to do something about us. They have already forgotten the good that we have done! I still stand by the fact that those motorcyclists got what they deserved."

"Well, things have certainly turned out the way we feared they might," said Old George. "I fear we may have to get used to these panicked reactions. I'm absolutely determined that we must carry on, but in a slightly more moderate and measured way."

"I think you might be right about that after all," said Big Puss as he finally got his breath back. "Today's revenge killings have made me much more cautious. I'll fall in line with your requests from now on, rein myself in a bit."

"That's the best news I've heard all day," said George with relief.

"Yippee!" shouted the assembled animals. "Three cheers for Big Puss, and welcome to the fold!"

Old George poured out a dish of milk and laced it with some rum. "There now, Big Puss, get that down ya!"

Big Puss didn't really like rum but appreciated the gesture and thought it would do no harm, so he licked the dish dry and thanked George for his kindness.

Chapter 19
A Decision to Visit Scotland

The next day the papers were full of events involving vandals and animals. The hospital outpatient departments were full of casualties. It was even reported in some areas that the police were finding their job easier than expected as so many animals had been bringing in criminals. In the past, so many instances of vandalism had gone undetected but now vandals were quite easily identifiable by the wounds animals had given them!

Old George and the animals were all pleased that the police had recognised the advantages of the attacks that were happening as a result of *Operation Upset*. Perhaps they would officially go on record and accept the animals and what they were doing, but there was no such luck yet. One report from the government was actually very worrying, as it said there was going to be an official inquiry in to the attacks and the positive reports before widespread government intervention followed.

Obviously, *Operation Upset* would have to either be sped up or stopped. The war cabinet had no intention of giving up now, however. They had nothing to lose by pushing on. It was a case of man winning, animal winning or man living in unison with animal. At the moment they felt that the animal kingdom was finding itself on the wrong end of the stick. In any event, Old George was too old to worry about a prison sentence. His life was nearing its natural end and he was determined to make a difference.

A meeting of the war cabinet was duly called, with the next course of action its subject.

Old George gave a summary of recent events from the radio and newspaper reports. He felt that their fate was in the balance but that they would be relatively safe provided the headquarters of their cabinet was not revealed to the public. Should that happen it would likely be fatal for all concerned. He continued on with the statement that they were about to enter an even more dangerous phase. It was his desire to commence attacks on television broadcasts. Radio was an invaluable and relatively wholesome endeavour, but he considered TV to be a social menace if it continued to broadcast the types of morally-dubious programming it did currently. Humans had to be put in a position where they would be forced to realign and rethink their entertainment and social lives for at least one year.

George considered that a short-lived temporary blackout of TV broadcasts would be of no benefit to the cause. In order to maintain a complete blackout of the broadcasts it would be necessary for animals to constantly damage power and transmission lines to prevent radio signals or cable-television being accessible.

"What about the Open University programmes?" wondered 605. "I heard the students in the animal house talking about it as being a good thing."

"A good thing for whom?" asked George. "There is so much unemployment among graduates. They'd do well to redirect their energies! A lot of the technology is damaging to life and the environment and what's more, many animals are used for their studies. No! They can either give up their programmes or move them to the radio."

"I heard of a lot of marriages breaking up over one or more parents getting involved in these extra studies," said 605. "It takes a lot of time and concentration. Some partners get annoyed when they are not the focus."

"Quite so," said Old George. "And the children in such families can also suffer. It takes a balanced partnership to withstand the strain."

"When do we start this step?" asked 700.

"As soon as possible, but this time we will have to consider contacting areas which have hitherto been untouched. That will help us reach more folk and, by spreading the message further afield, will help safeguard our identity."

"What do you mean?" asked Big Puss, only feeling half sober.

"Well, vandalism and mugging is uncommon in the more remote areas of Scotland and Wales, for example. Consequently, we have not had to call upon the animals in those regions. TV is available across all the land, so we will need to call on the wildcats and eagles who live in those areas to help our cause!"

"Hang on, hang on!" said 605. "What about the innocent people who live in remote areas of Scotland who want to take an Open University degree? Do you not think that our actions of destroying the TV network will be unfair? After all, they are unable to get to a university because of the remoteness of the area."

"Why are they living in such a region?" asked Old George. "I'll tell you why – because they like it! What good will a degree do? It won't make them any happier because they will find that they have a degree without practical experience. To get experience they have to leave home, and if they leave home, the best thing they can do is go to night classes and get day release from work. They will make more friends that way. No, I have decided! Does everyone agree?"

"Agreed!" shouted everyone but 605. "Down with television!"

605 looked around at the assembled animals and saw their enthusiasm. "Oh, alright!" said the rabbit.

"I must say this," said Wagtail. "Do you think we can get the necessary cooperation up in Scotland? After all, they don't know us up there and may have different ideas I think personal contact is always a good thing."

"It's more polite, too," added Owl.

"That's very true," said Old George. "I wouldn't like orders coming from unknown foreigners myself.

"But how can we make that personal contact?" asked Sparrow. "Send photo of us all sitting on top of a defeated vandal!" said Owl. "Be serious!" snapped Sparrow.

"I was…" replied Owl, quietly.

"We must go to Scotland," said 605.

"Go to Scotland?" exclaimed 700. "You must be joking!"

"No, I'm not. It would be the best thing for us, the most helpful and constructive."

"You know, I think it would," agreed Old George. "It would help us to assess where we need to attack and would ensure better cooperation. We will go to Scotland! We'll recruit support and boost our morale as well!"

Everyone became so excited at the thought of going to Scotland that no one paid any attention to the logistics of such an idea. During a more lucid moment it suddenly occurred to 605.

"How are we going to get to Scotland?" came the question.

"How are we going to get to Scotland?" laughed 700. "It's obvious! We're going to use the, the. Erm. Well, we're going to use the… George!? How are we going to get to Scotland?"

"You leave that to little old me!" said George in a confident tone.

"Well, that sounds excitingly mysterious," said 700. "I hope he doesn't expect us to walk, though."

"Or fly!" added Wagtail.

"I would never make it," said Sparrow with a concerned expression. "It's over twelve thousand miles to Scotland."

Old George laughed. "What school did you go to, my friend?"

"It's actually only about four hundred miles from here to Edinburgh," said Owl. "By road, at least. By wing it is only about three hundred."

"It's still a very long way to walk," said 700 glumly.

"Now don't you lot go worrying," said George. "Nobody is going to walk. Or fly! I hope."

"Can we all go?" asked 605.

"No," said George. "Someone will have to look after the cottage. The war cabinet will come but the others will have to stay. If too many go, we are going to look mighty strange crossing the frontier in to Scotland. They will think Cromwell is on the move again!"

"Will we have to prepare anything before we go?" wondered 605.

"Only sandwiches," said Old George. "And money, of course. I will go upstairs to get sufficient funds to keep us mobile and fed. With money, we can go anywhere and do anything."

Old George toddled off upstairs and soon returned with a wad of notes. "It's my last," he said. "Only my pension left after this is gone."

"Can we go now?" asked an impatient voice.

"Not yet," replied George. "I'll get some tomatoes and cheese and then we can get bread from the local baker. I'll make the sandwiches in the car."

"In the car!?" cried Owl. "What car? Are we going in a car? Yippee!"

"I had hoped to keep it a secret until the last minute," said Old George. "But I've only gone and blurted it out."

"So there really is a car?" asked 700.

"Yes, there is a car we can use," admitted George. "I don't like the damned things really but under the circumstances we are going to use it. We need it to help the cause. I only hope I can remember how to drive."

Old George beckoned to Owl. "Go and tell the others that we are leaving on a short trip and that the war cabinet will be away for a time. Tell them to behave and to look after things here."

"Will do," said Owl.

"The rest of the war cabinet, step this way!"

Chapter 20
The Car

The cabinet marched faithfully along behind Old George. They didn't know where they were going but the element of mystery made it all the more exciting. He took them out of the garden and down a lane, along a narrow path edged with escallonia and across a small field. On they continued, down another path with grass so long that 605 and 700 nearly disappeared from view. It looked as though it hadn't seen a living creature in generations! Eventually, they passed an old cottage without a roof and on the opposite side of that building they could see a large and intact house.

"Here we are," said Old George as he opened a rickety gate.

The house was very big and very old, with a crooked chimney and badly positioned tiles on the roof. The paintwork was in a dreadful condition, to say the least, and the garden was very overgrown with weeds – though one could still identify the pear trees and rambling roses in amongst the mess. There was an old sundial in the middle of the lawn which was overgrown with lichen and looked more like a strange, giant vegetable than a piece of ornate stone.

The war cabinet all thought the same thought, that this was a neglected place but somewhere that would be lovely and quiet to live!

Old George knocked at the door. The wood was dry and cracked, leaving the door hanging low on its hinges. 700 thought how easy it would be for the winds to get in. An old lady could be seen through the drooping door. She ambled towards the door, which was eventually opened.

"Why hello George! Fancy you turning up like this. Gosh it's nice to see someone. How are you getting on?"

"I'm fine, Mrs Lund. Really fine. And how is your arthritis?"

"Oh, not so bad you know, can't complain in this dry weather. It's the cold that starts me off! Now, what can I do for you today?"

The old lady had dark hair and her face was wrinkled with age. She still had beautiful blue eyes, which 700 thought exuded a sense of kindness. She was wearing a red jumper and a brown cardigan, a hearing aid perched in her left ear. On her feet she wore a pair of comfortable-looking slippers, trimmed with fur around the edge.

"Well, Mrs Lund," said George. "I've come about the car."

"Oh, the car! Fancy," smiled the Old Lady. "I thought you would never get around to using it. At least, I presume that you want to use it?"

"Well yes, I would like to head off for a few days."

"Oh my, what's got in to you? You must be feeling funny," she said. Old George laughed with a big smile.

"I'd best go and get the keys," said Mrs Lund.

"Aye, thanks. I'll probably need more than keys to start it," said George. "Then I'll get you a lot of the Lord's best wishes as well," said the kindly old lady with a grin.

Mrs Lund disappeared in to the house to get the keys and soon returned with a set of keys that looked as old as the house itself.

"There we are, George. I'm sure the doctor would be pleased to see you taking the keys!"

"Aye, that he would," replied George. "He was a kind soul. I'll never forget the day his will was read out. *To Old George, a faithful helper for many years, my car*. I could have fainted. I knew that he always appreciated my endeavours to keep it on the road and to keep it clean but to actually give me his car on his passing. Well, that was very considerate indeed. I never even really knew much about cars, it was all a bit trial and error like."

The Wolseley Hornet

"That may be, but it never let him down," said Mrs Lund. "He was ever so thankful for that."

"And fancy you, getting the house! That was real nice as well, I thought."

"Oh, it was! It saved me so much worry at the time, though I admit it's starting to deteriorate these days. It will last me until I go, though, that's for sure."

"Well, I must go. It may take some time to get the car started," said George. "I won't keep you. I see you have some company!"

"Oh, the animals! Oh, yes!" laughed George.

"You and your love of animals. You'll never change!" exclaimed Mrs Lund. "If you're heading away, I'll look after the cottage for you – and any pets."

George chuckled at the old lady's observation. She had known him a very long time indeed.

The war cabinet said a quick goodbye and went off to start the car. The garage was well-built and had a good, secure door. A window on each side of the structure allowed a lot of light in.

"Mrs Lund would be better living in the garage," remarked Sparrow. "Don't be cheeky," replied 605.

700 laughed, inwardly agreeing with Sparrow's assessment.

George also had to agree. "I wouldn't like to live in that old house," he said as he put a key in to the garage door's lock. After a brief struggle, the rusty old lock gave way and

110

the door was swung carefully back. An extremely old-looking navy blue and black car greeted them silently.

"Crikey!" exclaimed Sparrow. "What is that?"

"That, my unlearned friend, is a Wolseley Hornet. More than that, it was Dr Winterbottom's Wolseley Hornet!"

"But it is so old," said Sparrow in amazement. "It is surely older than you, George."

"Tripe! That, my dear *fellow-of-the-air* is a 1934 Wolseley. A very fine, if old, piece of British engineering."

"No wonder we have gone to the dogs," said Sparrow.

"What do you mean, *we*?" asked Old George. "You've got African blood in you.

You're not British."

"Is that right?" wondered Sparrow aloud, looking at 605 for help. "Yes, George is right! You are related to the beautiful African finches."

"Oh, golly! I didn't know that. That must be why I get so cold in the winter! Is that why I have such dark feathers as well?"

"Probably," said 700, not really sure of the answer.

"He's like the prime minister," said Old George. "Related to President Amin!" They all laughed, except Sparrow. He didn't think it was at all funny.

George opened up the car and lifted the bonnet. Everything was covered in dust.

The electric wires looked perished but the oil level was up to the right mark and the battery still had a good charge. He checked the petrol tank and found at least two gallons present.

They all looked at the tattered interior. The leather seats were dried out and cracked. They were of a design that was originally supposed to hold air, inflated cushions having been a fashionable trend at the time. The lever that advanced or slowed the ignition timing had been tied back with string. George remembered that it had a habit of moving with the vibration once the car was on the move but seemed to recall it never made much difference however it was set.

George was just about to turn the engine over with the starting handle when he remembered about the water in the radiator. He had drained it off years ago after the doctor had passed away in the hope that the radiator wouldn't corrode if it was kept dry.

He looked around in the hope of finding a watering can but could only find an old Wellington boot. He began to fill it with water from the tap inside the garage.

"Watch there are no socks in the welly," said Sparrow.

George spilt a great splash of water as he chuckled. "You silly devil, don't put me off!"

Eventually the radiator was full, the water overflowing out on to the garage floor.

"We are now ready for action and lift-off!" said George in a hopeful tone.

"Huh," said Sparrow. "Some hope of that. They won't let you in to Scotland with that old heap!"

George didn't have an MOT certificate, nor either a licence or insurance. He could hardly disagree with Sparrow on this one. *To hell with it,* he thought. *So what!*

With a firm grip, George cranked the engine's starting handle three times. He then switched on the ignition and was surprised to hear the electric fuel pump thumping away enthusiastically. *Ta-dah,* he thought. *The damn thing may just start by itself after all.*

He engaged the starter and the engine began to move. So did the car. It lurched forward, straight in to the remains of a potted plant that had been left in the garage.

George had forgotten to take the car out of gear.

He tried again and this time the engine fired in to life with a massive cloud of smoke belching from the exhaust. After some disconcerting bangs and farts the horses in the engine settled at a steady canter. The engine sounded like it was running as smoothly as a not too well-oiled clock but the exhaust smoke gradually cleared to a consistency more akin to cigarette smoke than that from an industrial plant. George was quite pleased with both himself and the old car. The battery had been renewed shortly before the doctor's death and the tyres had all been quite recent purchases as well. He could not envisage any further trouble.

Sparrow was less confident, though. "We'll never get there," he said. "As sure as fate they will stop you at the border."

"Go on with you! They'll think I am the Queen's *Keeper of the Pets,* going up to Balmoral," smiled George.

"Aye, that'll be right," said 700.

"More like a refugee fleeing from customs," said Owl, who suddenly arrived on the scene. "I told everyone that we are off on a wee holiday. They didn't seem much concerned."

"Good," said George. "Let's pile in and get back to the cottage. We'll make one final quick check and then go."

Chapter 21
Scotland, Here We Come

About an hour later, they had all organised themselves in to an expeditionary force. They bought the bread that they required from the bakers, made up the sandwiches and made their way to the motorway.

The car purred along quite nicely at, what was for the animals, a terrifying forty-five miles per hour. The back wheels were a little buckled because the wire spokes had loosened somewhat over the years so the old car went along the road waggling from side to side like a film star with an exaggerated swagger.

George vowed to get the wheels seen to.

"I feel sick," said Sparrow. "I want to get out."

"Here, take one of these," said George as he handed the bird a packet of Kwells motion-sickness tablets. "I brought these along, just in case."

Sparrow crushed the tablet in his powerful little beak and swallowed. "I feel better already," he said.

Old George grinned. *Must have been psychological,* he thought to himself. *Either that or the tablets work like dynamite on sparrows.*

The old Wolseley soon arrived at the Newport Pagnell junction of the M1 and with a deep breath George turned on to the slip road and waited for his turn to join the ranks of traffic. He was shitting himself at the thought of driving, or rather competing, with the big heavies of the road. Regardless, he found a gap in the traffic and emerged in to the stream of vehicles that were heading north. It was as though the stream of traffic had absorbed him, the Wolseley literally disappearing in the mass of metal carried by the M1.

Just up the motorway was a service station. Old George suddenly remembered that he needed to buy plenty of fuel so steered off the motorway and filled the car's tank with petrol. As he went to pay for it, he found the attendant laughing to himself about the old car.

"Had it converted from coal, then?" he asked. "No," replied George firmly. "From straw!"

"Good for you!" shouted Owl, his keen ears having overheard.

"You'll never get where you're going in that," said the attendant. "Not in a month of Sundays! They'll chew you up and spit you out before you even hit the M6."

"Not going via the M6," replied George, trying to remain polite. "Where are you off to, then?" asked the inquisitive attendant. "Scotland."

"God help you," said the attendant. "You'll be shot on sight up there. They get frightened of things they don't understand. Shoot first and investigate after, that's their attitude."

Old George took his change from the attendant's outstretched hand. Without another word to the attendant he walked back to the car and drove off in disgust.

They rejoined the M1 smoothly. God was really with them today! They passed the junction that would have led them to the M6 and continued northward, all the way until they joined the A1. On they went, constantly heading north until they reached the Tyne Tees tunnel, which was full of fumes and smoke.

Sparrow, Wagtail and Owl all began to cough. "I'm very sensitive to fumes," coughed Sparrow. "Me too," agreed Owl.

"And me," said Wagtail, wincing as he wiped his bloodshot eyes. "We'll soon be out," said George.

"Aye, out for the count," said Sparrow as he coughed again.

Sure enough, the lowest point of the tunnel was soon reached and the ascent began in earnest. The sunlight reappeared through the filthy gloom of the tunnel's 'air' and the toll booths loomed in to view. Old George got out his money.

"Do we have to pay?" asked 700.

"I'm afraid so," said George. "You can't partake of the Northumbrian vapours for nowt!"

"I think they should pay us for demonstrating that we can survive in their filthy fumes," said an irate Owl. "At least we have confirmed that it is safe for humans."

"I feel like a pit canary," said Sparrow. "That was worse than a shift down the mines."

George chuckled at Sparrow's sense of humour. He was a moan at a times but could be a very funny companion.

The toll attendant was soon paid and the group carried on towards Morpeth, past Flodden Field and then up to Coldstream and the Borders. The latter stretches were nice and quiet with very little in the way of traffic. The road was good with many straight stretches and nice, gentle bends. It was paradise to get away from the busy main roads and they stopped several times for sandwiches and the occasional pee. Owl excitedly set off to hunt a wild haggis during one stop but failed to find any. He returned very disappointed indeed.

"They are bigger than you anyway," said Wagtail. "You'd never lift one."

"And they have sharp teeth," said Sparrow.

"And claws that would tear you apart!" added 700.

"I see," said Owl. "I didn't know that."

"Oh, yes, very fierce and fiery they are," piped up George as he joined in with the joke. "Best keep away from them. Death to all owls, they are. Have heard some shocking stories, I tell you. Certain death, very painful!"

Owl kept a brave face but retreated inside the car, climbing on to the back seat in to a position he considered most likely to protect him from a possible wild-haggis attack.

After about twelve hours of driving the River Forth was finally reached. They pulled in to the large car park at the southern end of the road bridge and decided to sleep there for the night. The pair of bridges across the firth looked marvellous in the evening light. The railway bridge looking more like a silhouette without lights and the road bridge lit up like a fairy castle bedecked in orange. What a setting for a peaceful night's rest!

Chapter 22
Meet Starling Across the Forth

The next day was rather damp and misty. "What a start to our Scottish tour," mused Old George.

"Always wondered what a Scotch mist was like," said Owl intently. "Aye, min laddie noo ye ken," said 605.

Old George started the car and made his way towards the approaches of the bridge, where they would again have to pay a toll.

"Crikey, this is getting a bit much," said 700. "Every time we cross over or under a river, it would appear we have to pay! What's the reason?"

"Oh, the bridge was built with borrowed money," answered Old George. "Borrowed from whom?" asked 605.

"The government," said George.

"But surely motorways and so on are also built from borrowed money?" countered 605.

"Exactly," said Old George. "There is no logic behind the argument. The damn government are just after the revenue. Apparently, they argued at the outset that the bridge was a luxury for local Scottish traffic. I've never heard such rubbish. The M1 is a luxury, too. The government should make up its mind whether or not Britain is one country to be governed as such. Imagine the population of Kent having to pay to enter the north or west. They wouldn't tolerate it!

Forth Road Bridge

"The people of Fife and the north cannot effectively enter Edinburgh without paying for the honour. The bridge has to be crossed to go in and out, especially if you work in Edinburgh. According to the last report I read the debt will never be paid because the interest rates and maintenance costs take a large percentage of the money raised by the tolls."

"How many folk are employed to look after the bridge?" asked Sparrow.

"About eighty, eighty-five. I think," replied George.

"Is that necessary?"

"I think not. Why a bridge like this should be treated with such concern I'll never know. After all, it is only a dual carriageway. Why fuss over it? If people want to commit suicide then let them. Put the lights on the thing out and close the toll booths. Let the traffic flow as if it wasn't a special stretch of road."

"Oh, I suppose they want to keep people employed," said 700. "Aye, most likely," agreed 605.

Old George brought the car alongside a toll booth, paid up and began to cross on to the bridge proper. Just then, a large flock of starlings rose across their path. Old George wound down the window and stopped at the side of the road. The lead starling flew low and did a victory roll over the bonnet. His wing caught the glass-faced water temperature gauge which was situated at the front of the bonnet, it being common for cars of this age to have externally-mounted gauges like that.

"Bloody Hell," cried the starling. "A bit too close that time. Are you Old George?"

Old George looked surprised. "Er, yes," he said with a blank look of amazement. "Been gettin' yer messages and instructions loud an' clear," said Starling. "My squadron is stationed at the south side of the road bridge. Just about to lead them off to Rosyth and district for the daily forage. Glad to delay take-off to talk to you, though. Honoured to meet you in fact, Old George. We've certainly got those human blighters on the run! Spiffing good fun, what?"

"Oh, yes. Er, spiffing good fun," said George, trying to mimic Starling's RAF-inspired accent.

Starling & Squadron on the Forth Road Bridge

"Had some bloody good sorties in the last few weeks. Edinburgh Meadows was full of muggers until we organised ourselves on your instruction. The only trouble came from the *City of Edinburgh* squadron of my brethren. Didn't like us Fifers coming over to their city, despite the fact that we were there to help clean up the place. Not one mugger in the Meadows now. The devils wouldn't dare go near the place! The medical students, doctors, nurses, scientists can all go through the Meadows to university without fear now.

"At one time, you know, it was terrible for them. One poor scientist suffered brain damage after an assault in the Meadows one night. Never did recover. Poor fellow."

"A sad story," said Sparrow.

"How terrible!" added Wagtail with tears in his eyes.

"There was one particular case we dealt with," began Starling with another story. "One night this cheeky mugger came back for a second go despite our previous efforts to deter him. We were so annoyed that the whole squadron grabbed the blighter and flew off with him! We flew across Edinburgh to Corstorphine Zoo. We hovered for a while over the polar bear enclosure and then let him go. Dropped him straight in to the pond there, what an almighty splash he made when he fell!

"You should have seen the polar bears go. They tore him apart! Very sad though, really. The next day there was nothing left except a few fragments of femur. The keeper couldn't understand why the bears were off their food! We wouldn't do it again, though. No need to, really. Word got around and mugging almost stopped overnight. Some folk have short memories, though, so we have to show our colours now and again."

"I'm very glad you have only been so severe on that one occasion," said Old George. "We had a case down south where a cat overdid it and ended up on the receiving end of a retaliatory raid by the police."

"Oh, we had that too," said Starling. "But we were canny. We roosted at the radio station at Castleland Hill in Fife that night. The next night we moved to Dunfermline High Street, where as luck would have it, we happened to catch several vandals in the nearby glen. The squirrels told us about the trouble in the glen with some help of the peacocks and we were able to put those humans on the road to good citizenship!"

"Isn't that wonderful?" said Sparrow. "What cooperation between species."

"That's what I like to hear," said George. "In fact, we will need a lot of cooperation to deal with the next stage successfully."

"Oh, yes! The television business," exclaimed Starling. "We've heard about that."

Just then, a yellow van pulled up behind the Wolseley. The driver got out and approached Old George's door.

"Och min, ye canny park here! Noo git movin'!" Starling flew off hastily.

"Oh, sorry," said Old George. "I'm just going. Isn't it a nice view from here?"

"When yiv wurkit oan this brig fir fourteen year ye dinnae notice it laddie," said the relatively youthful creature to the very old man.

"I suppose you are right. Well, good day to you," said George. George moved off towards the northern side of the bridge.

"Oh, God," said 605. "We are very high up. I'm not sure that I would like to be a starling."

"Oooh, look at that railway bridge," exclaimed 700. It looks a lot stronger than this flimsy thing. I think I would much prefer to go across on the train!"

"How do the trains go up and down those big arches," wondered Sparrow. "Is it like a scenic railway?"

"They don't go up and down the spans, silly! They go through the middle. Can you see that central fence going right across the middle from the north to the south side?"

Everyone peered across and sure enough, they spotted the central fence. "Well, that fence borders the railway lines," finished Old George.

Just then, a train arrived on the scene and began to cross the railway bridge from South Queensferry across to North Queensferry.

"There you are," smiled Old George. "Perfect timing!"

"And proves your point!" said Sparrow.

The two bridges, road and rail

"Are there any islands in the Firth of Forth?" asked 700.

"Oh yes, there are one or two," said George. "There is Inchgarvie, Inchkeith. The Isle of May and Inchcolm. Oh and Inchmickery, Cramond Island."

"Inchmickery?" laughed Sparrow. "What a funny name!"

"Inchmickery mousery!" chuckled Owl.

"Oh, trust you to think about food," said Wagtail.

"Is that where Mickey Mouse lives?" asked Sparrow.

"Oh don't make me laugh any more," said 605. "You do make my ribs sore!" The little car began the descent to the north side of the bridge. Ahead of them, perched on the fence which borders the road, was Starling. He was facing the oncoming traffic with his starboard wing outstretched. He directed the Wolseley in to the kerb with his port wing.

"Looks like Madame Butterfly," cried Sparrow. "Oh shut up, you twerp," grumbled Owl.

The car pulled in to a lay-by and Starling flew down in to the open window. "Back again?" asked Old George.

"Yes, I felt that we had a lot more to discuss."

Just then, Owl decided to stretch his big wings. He launched himself from the window ledge and flew up and up and up. Suddenly there was a scream, repeated several times. Shadows passed back and forth over the car. Old George stuck his head out of the window and looked up.

"Good God!" he cried. "Owl is in trouble!"

Chapter 23
Rescue Owl

Squirrel anti-vandal lookout point

Sure enough, Owl was being attacked. Black-backed gulls were angrily engaging with him and he was having the fight of his life. As he dived, they dived. As he climbed, they climbed. They kept pecking at him with their sharp, menacing beaks. Owl turned upside down in mid-air and grabbed one of the gulls with his massive claws. The gull tried to struggle, twisting this way and that, almost throwing Owl out of the air. At last the gull twisted once too often and fell limp. Owl had broken its neck. He let the dead-weight go, the limp bulk of feathered meat fell over a hundred feet in to the river below.

Owl was clearly exhausted from his struggle. The other gulls kept up the chase but with slightly less enthusiasm than before. Some of them were more intent on going after the carcass of their now ex-colleague. To them, it was a free meal. After a few more minutes of chasing they dived off down to the point where the gull's body had landed. Owl attempted to get back to the car but his wings were damaged and failing fast. He began to lose height too quickly. Down and down he dropped, getting closer and closer to the treacherous water below. He knew that he would not survive the drenching, his feathers not equipped with the necessary waterproofing to keep him safe.

On the bridge, the occupants of the car grew increasingly anxious. They had seen everything.

"Oh, what can we do?" panicked Sparrow.

"Oh George, please help him!"

It was then that Starling took control. "I hope you don't mind, George, but I know the area. Let me take over!"

"Sure thing," said Old George. "Carry on!"

"Sparrow and Wagtail, fly to your friend. Escort him on the way down and mark where he hits the water," snapped Starling firmly. "George, drive me down to the pier in North Queensferry. We must get ourselves a boat!"

Sparrow and Wagtail flew off as Old George started the dash to the pier. There was no short cut, they had to drive in the opposite direction for about half a mile before they could turn back on to the old road down to the ferry. Eventually they turned down to the pier, the site of the old ferry and the place where the boats had plied their trade across the water in the days before the bridge had been built.

A fence barred the car's way but Old George trusted the weight of the car and drove straight through, swinging left and right between the many boats which were lined up on the pier. He jammed on the brakes but the car didn't stop where he wanted it to. It skidded on the damp seaweed that grew on the pier and ran forward over the toes of a funny little man.

"What the hell are you doing, driving like that?" asked the now-irate funny little man. "This'll cost you fifty pounds!"

An equally aggressive little woman came bouncing on to the scene at that mount. "Bloody old fool!" she cried, though George had to admit he could not be sure to whom the remark was addressed. "It'll cost you one hundred pounds, not fifty! That old sod never did have any money sense."

Old George gasped at the thought of giving his life savings to either of them, even though it was clear the old sod was worthy of some pity.

"Oh, bugger off," said George. "I've got trouble to deal with. I'll see you later!

Come on, Starling, let's go!"

"I'll impound your car!" shouted the funny old man. "Aye, that we will!" added the old trout.

Old George ran down to the water's edge and jumped in to an inflatable dinghy.

Starling followed and landed on the fibreglass rear seat as George tried to balance himself, almost but not quite falling over. The oars were fixed in to the rowlocks and were quite secure.

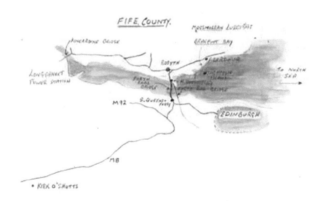

Map of the River Forth

"A lot better than the old heavy wooden boats," said Old George. "Are they?" said a voice from the pier. "Are they indeed?"

There was a loud hiss as a knife sank in to the rubber boat. The old trout had seen justice done and smiled as the arse end of the little boat began to disappear beneath the salty Forth. Sparrow took off and shat on the old bag, then returned in triumph to the more buoyant sharp end of the craft.

"I'll sue you in court!" shouted the old girl. "I'll have the last word!"

Before the echo of the threats had died away over the otherwise tranquil scene, she launched an almighty cry – along with a six-foot long boat hook. George realised she had clearly done this many times before as he watched her launch the hook with uncanny accuracy at a perfect forty-five degrees. It sailed through the air and came down on the starboard side of the boat, puncturing another of the rubber chambers that contained the air that kept the boat afloat; releasing it like a resounding fart.

George could see there were seven of these chambers overall. Two down, five to go as it were. Although he didn't doubt for one moment the old girl's prowess as a harpooner, he now felt that the stars were against him and that he should remain land-bound. He almost managed to forget about Owl's plight but not quite. No! He must overcome this temporary obstacle. Owl must be rescued and at any cost!

"Starling, what can we do about this old trout? She'll have to go, you know! We can't put up with this much longer, we need to get moving!"

By this time the old girl had hold of the painter, the little rope tied to the dinghy. "Got yer now," she uttered with a growl of satisfaction.

"Aye, she's got you now," added the funny little man. "Aye, that she has. You'll not get to see today."

"Oh, balls!" shouted Old George. It was most unlike George to use such language but under the circumstances he felt that something a little stronger than usual was called for. Time was pressing, they had to act quickly. Old George staggered off the firmly-held but slightly-deflated dinghy, at the same time thinking how similar to a fat bollard the woman looked. "A bollard on legs. Yes, that's what she is. A bollard on legs," he chuckled to himself.

"Aye, you can laugh," said the terrible twins. "Just you wait until get the bill for this lot."

George squeezed his way past the two on the pier, turned round and with one almighty heave pushed the pair in to the water. There was a tremendous splash and the biggest tidal wave that either George or the Forth had ever seen. It was nothing like the village pond in a storm! Much worse than that. He then grabbed a lifebelt and threw it in after them before jumping in to another dinghy. Starling joined him and they finally rowed off.

Ahead of them they could see two small flecks fluttering above the grey water. As they drew closer, they could see something like a glove bobbing in the water and a few minutes later they could make out the form of Owl. He was just managing to keep his beak out of the water.

They had arrived just in time to save him.

Old George stowed the oars and leaned out to grab Owl. He lunged at the mass of wet feathers that bore little resemblance to the fine bird that Owl had been prior to his ducking. George was lucky to be able to grab him on the first attempt and brought him onboard to dry off. There was an old scarf on the dinghy which George was able to use as a towel. Owl was going to be all right.

Wagtail and Sparrow landed on the boat and all five aimed for the shore. The funny old man and his female tornado had disappeared from the scene, presumably to dry off as well. Old George visualised her drying off in the heat of her own flames. The vision made him laugh.

The boat was soon tied up and they made a very quick dash for the car. To their surprise they made a clean and uninterrupted getaway!

"Thank God for that," said Starling. "We can talk about other things!"

Chapter 24
A Plan to Destroy the Forth Bridge

Longannet Power Station

Starling told Old George of man's plans to build a gas terminal on the site of a picturesque bay close to Aberdour on the north side of the Forth and expand an existing power station at Longannet. It was going to lead to more pollution because the oil companies had also planned for the siting of associated industries in the county. There was bound to be a leakage of highly inflammable gas at some point. In fact, there would always be a steady leakage from safety valves and the like during normal operation. The associated chemical industries would be particularly hazardous because dangerous fumes can be formed in the event of there being a fire. Even without a fire some of the fumes are obnoxious, especially to birds.

"It is us birds who get a raw deal," said Starling. "Can't we do something to stop the construction? Perhaps we could do something which would make them rethink?"

"That's what it is all about," replied George. "Making man rethink his plans."

"Can't we blow up the bridge?" wondered 605.

"What has the bridge got to do with it?" asked a very weak Owl.

"Well look," began 605. "If we destroy the road bridge Fife will be isolated, unless people use the Kincardine Bridge which is twelve miles away. The ferry boats don't run these days and industry doesn't seem to use the railways across the Forth much. Surely, without the bridge, they would have to rethink. Furthermore, if they thought that the place was a target for terrorists they would soon stay away."

Access beneath the bridge

Bridge under construction

"You know, you are right," said Old George. "Why wait until the gas terminal is built? It would be much easier to influence opinion now. But then, any form of power production is essential for hospitals and their patients, the elderly and most of the innocent and responsible population."

"What can we do?" asked Starling.

"Let's park the car and go back to the bridge. Let's have a shufti, followed by a serious decision to act with responsibility beneath the bridge arches."

Old George parked the car and the motley crew ascended to the level of the road which goes over the bridge. The stairs were tiring for George but eventually they made it and stood next to the north carriageway, next to a mound of earth which concealed a wooden door. It looked like an entrance to a mine and outside lay a very large wooden reel. On the reel was wound a great length of electric cable. It was clearly very strong cable capable of carrying an extremely high voltage.

Starling asked George what the funny-looking mound of earth was.

"Oh, that is a power-house," said George. "Very high voltage, I think. Hmmm. I wonder." He thought for a minute or two, the others watching the gears grinding away in his mind. "Look, I have a very good plan."

"Yippee! I like your plans," said Sparrow. "And I," agreed 605.

"Me too!" said 700.

"Now look here, my friends," said Old George. "If we attach that cable to the power-house and the other end to the road bridge, then switch on the power, the wires holding the bridge up should melt."

"Melt?" asked Sparrow.

"What do you mean, melt?" wondered 700 in unison.

"Well look at it this way," began Old George. "If we wire up the bridge like I said it will turn in to one big electric fire. It is all metal except for the foundations and roadway. It will get hotter and hotter until it melts."

"I like that," said Starling. "I'll lose my roosting site but I still like it."

"Good, then let us proceed," said George.

"Will it be illegal?" asked 700.

"I would think so, but I think it was illegal to put it up in the first place. It has destroyed the quietness and house prices in Fife. A lot of people will thank us in the end."

"I'm sure they will," nodded 605.

"There's only one problem," said Starling. "They have six television cameras aimed at various points on the bridge. They are probably watching us now."

"Get your starling friends," said Old George, "And give them some nice and fresh fertiliser. Erm, the cameras, I mean, not your friends."

"I knew what you meant," smiled Starling with a twinkle in his eye. Starling quickly rounded up the squadron and the bombardment began soon after.

When Old George was satisfied that the cameras were covered, he carried a hacksaw from the car and a knife in his pocket, the kind that had several blades folded into the handle. He took the saw blade and removed the outer sheath of the wire that was on the drum. The strands within the insulation gleamed yellow in the sun. "Now we need to unwind enough wire to lead twice from the bridge to the power-house," he said.

"Why twice?" wondered 700.

"Positive and negative leads," said George.

700 leaned over to 605 and whispered, "What's positive and negative?"

"Don't know," said 605. "As long as he knows then I don't care too much."

"Oh, agreed, agreed," nodded 700, none the wiser.

Old George tried to pull the wire off the enormous drum but the thickness and weight of the cable made it a wasted effort. "Get me a horse," he huffed. "I need a horse!"

"Do you want a saddle as well?" asked Sparrow. "No, just a horse," laughed George.

"Get him a horse!" shouted Sparrow, though to whom was not entirely clear. "Without a saddle!"

"I can't get a horse in broad daylight," said Starling. "We will have to rest up until nightfall."

"OK, well let's discuss attacking the TV aerials and transmission stations in that case," said Old George. "Any suggestions, anyone?"

"We could interfere with maintenance by well, you know, bombarding the masts," suggested Starling.

"Excellent," said 700. "Isn't that a good, non-aggressive way of working!"

"The men will still feel like shooting you, or anybody else who mucks on their masts," said 605.

"That's for sure," said Starling. "They don't like us for that."

"We also need rabbits to burrow beneath the aerials. If the mining is done properly the masts should capsize without injury."

"I could organise that," said 700.

"No, you stay here," said Old George. "The wild rabbits will have to be handled carefully. The personal touch, you know."

"George, aren't the aerials cemented in to the ground?" asked 605.

"They probably are but I am sure the hardy Scottish rabbits will be able to burrow below the depth of cement."

"Oh, that's good," said 605. "You and I could always help them in case of difficulty. Are the aerials far from here or do we have a lot of driving to do?"

"They are situated close to the M8 motorway. At least, the ones which cover this area are situation over there." Starling said as he raised a wing and pointed in the general direction of the masts, roughly south-west of where they stood.

"Good," said Old George with relief. "We can supervise one of the local operations and the animal kingdom can communicate the successful procedure to the operations elsewhere."

"You are very confident that we are going to succeed," said Wagtail with glee. "We *must* succeed," said Old George. "If it is the last thing we do, we must succeed! If man returns to his old habits and ways after we are finished then I will feel that things must be destined that way, but at least we will have done our best."

Chapter 25
My Kingdom for a Horse

The day wore on with very little further activity other than vain attempts by the bridge maintenance staff to clean the TV camera lenses. Their headquarters were positioned at the south side of the bridge, so they had started their unenviable task at the south side. It was obviously going to be a day or two before all of the cameras would be back in action but even then, Starling and his squadron could be called to arms again.

As soon as darkness fell, Old George asked Starling to show him where he could get a horse. Starling knew of three horses which were fielded very close by, just to the east of the road bridge. He beckoned to Old George to follow him.

"Look, I think you should sit on my shoulder," said George. "I can't move as fast as you and furthermore you may bang in to something in the dark."

Sparrow's face went red with embarrassment when he remembered his own earlier night-flight.

"You are quite right," said Starling. "I'll sit on your shoulder!"

The would-be horse thieves made their way down the steps on the east side of the bridge and then crossed the road at the bottom. In the orange glare from the lights of the bridge they could see a small field, in which there were a number of ponies and horses.

"Take your pick," said Starling, pointing to the horses that were happily munching away on the rather short grass.

They made their way in to the field and walked over to the nearest pony. The animal looked up at the night visitors with a blank stare.

"He looks awfully big close up," muttered Sparrow.

"Wouldn't like to get on the wrong side of him," said 700 with a nervous voice. "Now then, steady old boy," said George, approaching from the front of the horse. "How would you like to help us tonight, eh?"

Old George put his hand in his pocket and removed a rich tea biscuit which looked like it had been through the Battle of the Somme.

"There now, me old boy. Have a biscuit."

A rich tea biscuit? That's the surest way to lose friends, thought 700. *Glad I'm not the horse. Old George could have offered the nag something more delectable.*

The horse had obviously never been spoiled by over-rich feeding because he munched in to the remains of the dead biscuit as if it were the highest-quality caviar.

"Thanks awfully," said the horse in the most aristocratic of tones. "Thanks awfully muchly. You are a kind fellow, what?"

"Eh, well, yes, yes that's quite all right," stammered Old George.

Old George reacted to the aristocratic nag in true servile manner. It was a conditioned reaction typical of those with his breeding and background. The interaction between the two was really quite a moving experience to observe.

"What can I do for you?" asked the nag.

Old George stammered and stuttered. He was clearly a bit thrown by the unexpected encounter. He hadn't anticipated running in to a nag of such culture and high breeding so far north of the English border.

"Take your time," said the nag. "Gather yourself together first and then we can get down to the nitty-gritty, what?" The creature put his aristocratic neck downwards towards the far-from-lush scrub. He began to eat the herbage by his hooves. After a few mouthfuls he obviously considered that Old George should now be in a fit condition to carry on a sensible conversation.

"Well now, you were saying," prompted the nag.

"Er, could we borrow you for a time?" asked George.

The aristocratic nag pushes the door

"Borrow me? But my good chap, what do you mean, borrow me? At this time of night? A bit much don't you think, coming up to a chap and blurting out that you want to borrow him."

Old George began to wish he had never bothered. He began to get hot under the collar. Owl began to see his companion's plight.

"I say, old chap," said Owl to the nag. "What my friend really means is could you help us in our hour of need?" Owl recalled the odd Churchillian sentence which he knew would span the gap between them. It worked wonders.

"Never has so little been asked of so few by so many, what Haw, haw, haw!" uttered the nag in broad Etonian. "Yes, of course. Be damned pleased to oblige, what. You're from the Harrow area, aren't you? Recognise the accent anywhere."

"Er, well," Owl had to think fast. "Yes, yes of course. How did you guess? What a damned observant fellow, horse! Part of your breeding, I suppose." said the bird as he tried to butter up the much-bigger creature.

"Well, yes. Born in me, I suppose," said the nag with a superior air.

Owl gulped at the lies he had told. If only the nag knew that he had been educated in the woods of Middle Wallop and Bedford.

"Spout away," continued the nag. "How can I help?"

Old George, Sparrow, 700 and the rest went to great lengths to explain what everything was about. The aristocratic nag was in full agreement until Owl tactfully mentioned the desire for a hand to execute manual labour.

"Well, it's been nice talking to you," said the nag. "Hope you are successful."

"Oh, come on," said Owl. "You can't let the team down. We need your leadership. After all, what would Eton say if they found out that you had backed down from a challenge which had been taken up by an old Harrowvian, what?"

"Oh, well, of course I was only joking. Just testing your reaction, you know. Old trick of mine. Let's you find out more about people, how they react. Of course, I'll come along to keep you right."

"That's absolutely fine, damn splendid," said Sparrow as he tried to cover up his almost vermin-like background.

Owl flew up on to the nag's head and acted as a night-light of sorts. George hefted himself up on to the horse's back, after excusing himself of course. The remainder joined Old George on the non-existent saddle. With a gentle *gee-up* the journey back to the power-house began, Owl adeptly guiding them in the gloom.

They soon arrived back by the door and everyone dismounted.

"Come over here, Horse," said Old George. "I want to show you what I want to do." George pointed out that he wanted the drum of wire placed on its side while he unwound a sufficient amount to reach to the bridge and back. He felt that it would be a better approach than to try and roll the drum, which would have risked a runaway situation. He wanted the horse to lean against the drum until it fell over.

The aristocratic nag wasn't too pleased about this but did eventually position himself with his blunt end against the wooden side of the drum. Old George got a rope from the car and tied it on to the side of the drum opposite where the nag was going to apply his posh arse. Owl positioned himself so that he could see both the pusher and the puller.

"I'll guide the operation from here," shouted Owl. "Everyone ready?"

"Best cheek forward!" bellowed Sparrow to the nag.

Everyone else not actively involved moved out of the way. "Right!" shouted Owl. "Push and pull, now!"

The old man strained on the rope and the nag spread his backside along the wooden slats on the opposite side. The drum rose up on one edge. Gently at first, then faster. Three inches, a foot, two feet…

"Look out, it's going over!" cried Owl. Suddenly the reel hung, poised as the centre of gravity lay through the point of contact with the ground.

"Push, push! Just a little more!"

The old Etonian did just that and the drum went crashing to the ground. A large cloud of dust rose from the area of ground surrounding the fallen drum. It wasn't that they could see the dust in the orange light but they certainly felt it. Everyone began to sneeze.

"Yippee!" shouted Wagtail. "Good oh! Well done old *hawse!*"

"It was nothing really, anyone could have done it. Well, not just anyone, but anyone from Eton or Harrow. What say you, Owl?"

"Couldn't agree more, old fellow," said Owl in an amiable tone. "Well done!" Old George stroked the horse and thanked him for all the help he had given. "Oh, just one more thing before you go," said Old George. "Could you help to pull the cable in to position?"

Horse agreed to help finish the job of cable-laying. "And what about breaking the door of the power-house?" he asked.

"Good forward thinking," said Owl. "You can tell he comes from the right school. Always shows in the end. Can't hide these things for long."

"'ark at him," said 700 to 605.

"Push the door down if you can," said George.

The nag moved towards the door and as with the drum he advanced rear-first. He began to rhythmically bump against the frail door, which soon gave way under the weight of the piece of equine rump steak.

"Now, to bare the wires and connect up," said George with a mote of relief.

Chapter 26
The Destruction of the Forth Bridge

The cable was duly cut and laid out between the power points in the building and the nearest metal girder of the bridge. Old George threw the mains voltage switch. The lights on the bridge went out. He was now unable to see anything. He quickly threw the switch again and the lights came back on.

"I'll have to use a torch," shouted George. He looked around the power-house and found a tool box in the corner. Inside the box was a small torch. He tried the little switch on the barrel of the torch and a weak glimmer of light appeared from the bulb. They were in luck.

By this time, Old George's hand was shaking with worry and excitement. The cold air inside the power-house didn't help, either. There was a rather damp, oily smell about the place. Kind of sickly like. He fumbled with the main switch again and the lights went out for the second time. Owl held the torch under his wing while Old George worked away. The old man found little difficulty in making the contacts. After all, the wire was so thick that the delicate touch was hardly needed.

"Right, everyone outside!" shouted George. "Get behind the bushes above the power-house and stay out of sight."

Old George saw that everyone was clear before he threw the switch. The bridge lights went on for a second or two and then flickered out, having blown due to the short circuit that George had caused.

The traffic still flowed gently across the bridge, perhaps one car every two minutes. Old George worried about the possible consequences when the full effect of the electric charge would begin to take hold. He declined to observe from the same hiding place as the rest.

The saboteurs crouched behind the bushes and waited to see what would transpire. Everything to be quiet and peaceful. They were surprised that no one had come across to investigate the loss of lighting. A boat's siren sounded in the Forth, sounding rather eerie in the darkness, although there was still a fair amount of light reflected from the town of South Queensferry. Obviously the black-out was localised on the bridge.

Suddenly, a low humming noise was heard. The volume of the noise rose from barely-audible to quite loud.

"Probably a helicopter," said Old George in answer to the unasked question that everyone was thinking about. It was no helicopter, however, because it soon became apparent that it was too steady and close to be anything other than the bridge. The bridge itself was making the humming noise. There was a strong smell of burning paint. It got stronger and stronger, and after a few minutes the smell began to sicken the sensitive aves in the group, so Old George advised them to fly to a better vantage point. In actual fact, he now thought that it would be wiser for him to get in to the car and seek a better viewing point away from the immediate area.

"Come on, everyone," he shouted. "Let's go! Horse, thanks very much for everything. You had best go back to your field but keep clear of the bridge."

"Good bye, everyone!" shouted Horse. "Awfully good show. Spiffing good fun, what?"

George and his colleagues jumped in to the old car and made off. They travelled for about one to two miles before they came upon a suitable point from which to observe the bridge. Old George switched off the engine and they all looked towards the darkened bridge. By this time the black silhouette had turned in to a faint orange colour. The bridge was beginning to glow in the dark. As the glow increased in intensity, they could see smoke rising from the burning paint on the steel cables. The saboteurs sat, staring with amazement.

The demolished bridge

"Who would have believed it?" said Old George.

"I do hope your squadron has got off all right, Starling," said Wagtail. "I'm sure they have. They would have moved soon after the noise started."

The bridge steadily changed colour from orange to bright yellow and then bright white. They could see a queue of cars gathering at the south side of the bridge.

Unfortunately the north side in the region of the power-house was out of sight. In any case, all the maintenance crews would be at the south side so the bridge would just have to keep getting hotter and hotter. Only immediate access to the power supply would prevent the bridge from reaching melting point.

Meanwhile, at bridge HQ, everyone and everything was at panic stations. The tar was melting on the bridge and all traffic had stopped. The whole of the bridge was glowing like one big ornamental electric fire. The road surfaces began to slide from the raised centre of the bridge towards either end. Only a tracked vehicle could have crossed such a mess but either way, nobody would have had the courage to cross to the north side even if such a vehicle had been available. The telephones were out of commission. The whole of the HQ's emergency services were useless.

The situation was made worse by the fact that the Royal Navy had moved out of Port Edgar, which was close to South

Queensferry. They could not be called upon to help. In any case the bridge was now at such a high temperature that the metal was beginning to twist out of shape. The central towers began to move in towards the centre of the bridge as the end arcs of supporting cables began to expand and stretch. The towers were losing their strength.

Suddenly, the south tower twisted to one side as the eastern support cable finally melted. It fell like a long piece of fluorescent tubing in to the water below. There was an almighty bang as the steam spontaneously produced by the white-hot cable impacting the water tried in vain to rocket from beneath the metal to the surface of the water.

Bubbles of hot steam came rushing to the surface like the air rushing from a sinking ship. The bubbles took on a bright, iridescent glow as they fought their way to the surface through the grey-black water.

For a few more seconds the damaged structure lay dormant like some large monster in the final throes of death. Finally both towers began to bend about twenty feet above the top of the stone formations. With a resounding crash the two towers met, remained motionless for what seemed to be an eternity and then fell in unison in to the water. The rising steam obscured everything for a few minutes and then there was nothing. The entire bridge and its carriageways had disappeared. There was only the approach roads left to indicate that there had been a bridge at that spot.

Old George looked at everyone in the car. "We had better get away from here," he said with a feeling of immense guilt.

Chapter 27
I Need a Radio

The car moved off without a murmur from the occupants. They all sat there with their thoughts, not wanting to laugh or discuss anything. After a mile or two Starling broke the silence.

"Look, George, you must be worrying. Why not pull in for the night and have a good rest?" suggested Starling.

"Oh, I wouldn't be able to sleep. Need to keep moving."

"Well look," replied the bird. "Two things must be seen to. One, we need to know what is happening in the outside world. We need a radio. Two, we need to contact the rabbits at Kirk O'Shotts where they have the TV mast. It follows that if we are going to drive around all night then we should seek a radio and finish close to Kirk O'Shotts." Starling had spoken with such authority he'd sounded like a school ma'am.

"That sounds very sensible," murmured 605.

The others all agreed so Old George had no option but to go along with the plan. "OK," he said. "We will do that. Starling would you please direct me to the nearest garage? We may be lucky enough to find a very cheap radio. I'm thinking of the miniature ones which fit in to the palm of the hand. They only cost a few pounds."

"OK," said Starling. "Turn left at the next T-junction and then take the second left. You should find a garage on the left, which is one of the few in Scotland that stays open all night."

George did as he was told and sure enough found a garage exactly where Starling had indicated. George stopped the car and topped up the petrol tank. He then went in to the shop, paid for the fuel and began to seek his radio. The shop was

147

full of tourist rubbish, the sort of things that people buy on impulse. They seemed to have everything but radios. Old George decided to ask at the cash desk.

"Do you have any radios, please?"

"No, sir," came the positive reply. "It's after dark and you are in Scotland." The assistant laughed with a tone that suggested Scotland was not yet out of the candle and paraffin era.

In the background George could hear a radio playing the latest bottom-twenty hits. He cringed at the thought of the non-musical cacophony that must make up the top twenty hits.

"Is that your radio playing?" asked George. "Ye, wan a buy it?"

"Yes, why not? That is, provided it can talk as well as play that rubbish."

"That's no' rubbish, mate, that's good hot music man. Yah, yah, yah, chee, chee, chee."

George was convinced that the human Afghan Hound behind the noise was an escaped gorilla but that was beside the point. He had to get hold of a radio so he decided to put up with a few minutes more of the odd utterances.

"Seriously, I want to buy the radio. What's your price?" enquired the old man. "Five quid," replied the gorilla, holding up a rather battered example of a descent of Logie Baird's original listening device. Someone had added an external speaker to the main guts of the thing, which made it looked like a mongrel cross reproduced from the mating of a radio and telephone.

"Five quid for that time bomb," said George in a raised voice, trying to use some sales psychology. "I'll give you two quid. You can keep the external stereo fittings."

Even to Old George the device showed no resemblance to a stereo but the old man thought that he had better not upset the young swine at this advanced stage of the diplomatic détant.

"Oh no," said the budding tycoon. "It'll lose its value if I separate the parts. You will have to take it with the stereo."

Whereupon he began to unwind ten feet of loudspeaker wire. George wondered what was going to happen next.

The gorilla placed the external speaker on the counter and then the nerve centre of the complex system on a shelf above the till. He then proceeded to seek a station which was likely to emit noises sought by Old George.

"There we are. Hear that, man? Listen to those trumpets and that piano. First they play over here," he pointed to the quivering speaker which was almost jumping out of its paper cone. "And then over here."

He had no sooner pointed to the crackling radio when it fell off the shelf and crashed to the floor. The subsequent swan song only lasted five seconds. It was a very moving experience.

"Lordy, it's broken," uttered the apparently devout-Christian gorilla. "You'll have to pay for it now, you old bat. Why didn't you take it in the first place? It's all your bloody fault."

George understood the reason for the young buck's outburst. After all, *Old George* had once been *Young George* and still hadn't forgotten the strains of being young.

"I'll give you four pounds provided you get it going without the use of the external speaker," said George.

The gorilla fumbled with the silent piece of electronic plastic. First, the speaker was ripped off and thrown to the floor like a temperamental surgeon might do when executing his umpteenth prostatectomy of the day.

"That bugger won't cause any more trouble," he muttered in to his denim shirt.

With the inside of the communication system open to the air and wedged on his chest he proceeded to prod and pull, cough up phlegm and turn screws with his dirty broken nails. Suddenly, the thing burst in to life only to fade in to nothing, as if the band which had been playing had been tied to the arse end of a moon rocket. There was nothing sudden about the silence, it was all very gradual and proper like.

That thing is showing a touch of experience and practice, thought George. *The damn thing had obviously done it on many earlier occasions.*

After a few more minutes of grunting and groaning the gorilla looked up at George and without uttering a word launched the receiving device in the direction of the partly-open door. His aim and ability to throw things was not up to the standard of his earlier emotional outburst. However, nobody is perfect at all things.

The radio landed in the middle of the air-freshening *Dolly Danglers* and proceeded onward in a downward direction, taking with it the stand on which the aforesaid articles had been hung.

"Take the bloody thing!" shouted the irate and impatient gorilla.

George did as he was bid. He objected to the country's youths giving him orders but on this occasion, he could see a distinct advantage in obeying.

He bent down to pick up his present, shook the thing and put it in to his pocket. He had no sooner removed his hand when suddenly his pocket began to play the pre-news jingle. Old George could only think that he had got a bargain and had better leave while the gorilla was still in a benevolent mood.

The transmissions were still coming through when George was leaving the forecourt. He related his experiences to his animal colleagues who all agreed that things had worked out well for him.

"Listen," shouted 700. "Oh do listen, the news summary is about to begin."

The voice of the radio finished the sports commentary and commenced summarising the day's happenings.

"A tragedy of mammoth proportions has today occurred in Scotland. The Forth Road Bridge has collapsed in to the Firth of Forth. The government has called for a thorough inquiry. The police are also concerned about certain mysterious aspects of the case. Apparently, sabotage cannot be ruled out at this early stage in investigations."

Old George fumbled in his pocket in an attempt to switch the radio off. The voice in the pocket went silent.

"At least the thing has a working on-off switch," he murmured.

"Dear me," said 605. "They will be after our blood without delay if they discover that we had anything to do with that lot."

"They sure will," agreed Owl.

"I don't know so much," said 700. "We're hoping that they will be so pleased with their new way of life around these parts that they may even decorate us."

"Oh, they will decorate us all right," chimed Sparrow. "With a wire cage!"

"Yes, I'm inclined to agree with you, Sparrow," said Wagtail. "I reckon we will be sold on the open market after this little escapade."

"Or served on toast to the Frenchies," said Owl.

"Hot buttered toast at least, I hope," said Sparrow with a certain amount of glee. "Of course, of course. Hot buttered toast, none the less," added Old George, trying to forget his responsibilities. "I think we had better be careful from now on. If they associate our little car with this episode then we will soon be in the clink."

"I think we should get to Kirk O'Shotts as soon as possible, get the next stage organised with the rabbits and make our way home," muttered Owl somewhat reservedly. "The excitement is getting a bit too much for me on top of my dunking."

Without saying a word, Old George started the car and proceeded to find a quiet place to park for the night. They eventually found the Kincardine Bridge, which was now the nearest point for crossing the Forth.

"Thank God nobody has sabotaged this bridge," said Sparrow.

Nobody replied to Sparrow's comment. They were now too tired to talk or listen. The car wound its way off the main road and in to an open field. Old George swung the vehicle around beneath a hedge and switched off the engine and lights. He then settled down for a peaceful night, although he felt within himself that he would be doing more thinking than sleeping.

Chapter 28
An Encounter with Porridge

The next morning dawned just as all mornings tend to. Unfortunately, this particular dawn was not heralded by any impressive visible elevation of the sun. To be quite blunt about it, it was pissing cats and dogs; not an uncommon occurrence during the summer months in bonnie Scotland. It was sufficiently irritating to provoke rather blue-language statements from Sparrow about just how heavy the rain was coming down!

"Jesus wept! Not again, that's all we need," grumbled Owl. "I've just got myself dry after yesterday's dip and now it's going to happen again. My feathers are going to look like an old rag before I get back."

"Never mind," said Starling. "When you are wet you make a good *pu'-through* for a rifle."

"What does that common Scottish crow mean?" asked Owl, trying to look like he was only pretending not to know.

"What, you mean the definition of a *pu'-through*?" asked 605. "Yes," said Owl.

"A pu'-through," butted in Old George, "Is, as I understand, a common expression in Scotland for a pull-through. That is to say, a mop on a stick."

Everyone except Owl had heard enough. They all burst out laughing at the thought of a water-drenched Owl stuck on the end of a stick.

"A mop on a stick," continued George, "Which is then pulled through the barrel of a gun to clean it."

The roars of laughter could be heard miles away as everyone imagined old Owl being rammed bum-first (or last, it didn't really matter) up the barrel of a twelve-bore.

Even old Owl had to laugh in the end. He also considered, in all fairness, that he would look highly comical disappearing up the barrel of a shotgun. They all laughed so much that the tears began to flow.

The laughter eventually died away and more serious thoughts filled their minds. Food, for example. Old George opened the door of the car and let the birds and rabbits out to forage. Twenty minutes later, they all returned in ones and twos, having had their fill.

"Where is the nearest restaurant?" asked Old George.

"Off the M8, on the way to the TV mast," answered Starling. "I'll show you."

"I'll freshen up there and then we can go ahead to meet the wild rabbits of the neighbourhood."

George started the car and away they went. At the motorway restaurant George consumed a good breakfast of fried eggs and bacon. He finished off with two large cups of tea.

"Wid ye like oanie purrich tae finish ye aff?" asked the very attentive waitress. The fullness in George's stomach had already reached the second button from the top of his shirt. He thought it wiser to refuse the hardly-irresistible offer.

"Er, no thanks, dear. I've had enough for just now." Her appearance at this early hour of the day didn't exactly inspire confidence as to her state of hygiene. Oh, she wore a cap on her head alright but most of her unkempt hair hung like vines in a jungle film. At any moment Old George expected Tarzan to come swinging round the nape of her neck.

"It's gid for ye!" came the motherly voice. She didn't look old enough to have experienced whether the oatish plaster had any long-term nutritional value or not.

"I'm sure it is very good for a wet morning such as this but I really am full," said George, getting a wee bit fed up. Had he been in England he would have been a *little* fed up, but when in Rome…

"Aw gaw on wi ye!" barked Mary, Queen of Scots. "Ye kin aye fun room fir suc a fine dish as the purrich. All ginn an git ye sum."

At this stage George felt that he had three options open to him. He could either accept and suffer, run as fast as possible to escape but no doubt fall in doing so, or do something that would not be in keeping with his gentle upbringing.

"Well, give me a small portion then," said Old George with reluctance. "Only small now, not too much."

"Thon's the spirit!" came the cheery reply.

George was convinced that she must be the heiress to the Scott's Porage Oats fortunes. At least by thinking this it took his mind off the other possibility, that she had been given a bollocking for making too much *purrich* the previous day.

Within seconds, the gastronomic delight of Scotland arrived. She removed her thumb from the edge of the hot, seething mess and wiped the side of the dish with the corner of her pinnie. It reminded Old George of Polyfilla. The similarity between the two preparations was amazing to the extreme.

The answer to a do-it-yourselfer's prayer, thought George as he downed the first teaspoonful.

Boadicea's unseen eyes hadn't missed the most important ritual of purrich- eating. "Yiv firgotten the salt!" she bellowed.

George gulped. He knew that if he didn't add salt, she would do it for him. He reached for the condiments and selected the bottle with the single hole in the top. He noted that the other bottle also only had a single hole in the top, but it was clearly a pepper container that had lost its original lid.

"Noo be liberal wi' it," she barked. "Dinnae be feart!"

Old George placed his finger over the hole and pretended to be as liberal as she had directed.

"Nah, lik this!" she said, grabbing the salt bottle from Old George's grasp, whereupon she began to shake the contents of the bottle all over the purrich. And indeed, all over the table, Old George and the floor.

"Noo then, try that!" she ordered. "Get tore in!" Tarzan's mate stood back and waited for Old George to *get tore in*.

He took one mouthful, moved it round his mouth – and spat it out. The force of the blast made Tarzan's friend reel on her feet. George's eyes cleared and in the near distance he could see what looked like a wet plaster cast of a woman.

"Oh, I am sorry," cried George. "It's my complaint, you know. Hiatus hernia.

Comes on all of a sudden. Dear me, look at you. I am sorry."

The bionic purrich smiled and fled towards the lady's loo. George made a hurried exit to the waiting car.

"You look flushed," said Owl on seeing Old George's red face. What's wrong?"

"Purrich poisoning!" blurted George, at the same time putting the car in to motion.

"What's that?" asked 700.

"A rare, localised disease. Only the strong survive."

"Is that so?" asked Wagtail with a look of doubt.

Owl just blinked.

Chapter 29
Rabbit the Bruce

Rabbit the Bruce

The four-wheeled menagerie soon arrived at a suitable point for the meeting with the wild rabbits. Starling told George to wait in the car while he flew off to make contact. After some time, Owl spotted a fleck of black in the sky.

"Here he comes!" he shouted with excitement.

Moving up and down beneath the area of sky through which Starling was flying could be seen numerous little animals.

"Starling is bringing the rabbits. Yippee, yippee!" shouted Owl, jumping with joy.

Sure enough, as they came closer Old George could see the army of rabbits. "Thirty in number! No, forty. No, oh my," said a started George. "Seventy at least!"

"Here we are," said Starling as he landed on the window ledge of the car. "Your demolition squad wishes to meet you."

"Hello, George. Pleased to make your acquaintance," said a large buck. "I'm Rabbit de Brus, or to use the more modern spelling, Rabbit the Bruce. Just call me *The Bruce*."

"Very pleased to meet you," said George. Old George knew from his history lessons that anyone in Scotland with a title like *The Bruce* had to be respected. This bun was obviously of noble stock.

"Ooh, look at his muscles," said 605 in a low voice. "Fair makes my ears quiver!"

"I hope that is the only thing that quivers while he is around," said 700, feeling rather jealous. "We don't want any more passengers on the way home."

605 blushed at the thought of returning home with a litter of young. "Ooh, he is nice, though. What a cultured voice, too."

The Bruce looked towards a burly, older-looking buck. "Get the men into line!" he bellowed.

"Yes, sir!" said the burly rabbit.

In a matter of seconds the rabbits were lined up in seven rows of ten. In all there were actually seventy-two rabbits in the Scottish army.

"Stand at ease!" ordered Burly.

"Stand easy!" came the following instruction. The rabbit army stood in relaxed posture.

"My men are ready," said *The Bruce*. "Starling has explained your intentions and I agree with you that something has to be done. We don't have the freedom that we should have around here. We want that TV complex removed from here."

"Good," said George. "I was dreading that you may not cooperate."

"Well, I don't usually cooperate with the English but I think we are fighting a common cause in this instance."

"I think we are. This is what I would like you to do," said Old George. "It will be necessary for the rabbits to undermine the TV masts throughout the country. This will be a mammoth task which will require a large mining force. The whole operation will be made more difficult by the presence of concrete foundation pads beneath the structures. It will not be possible to remove the concrete, so the mining will have to proceed to a depth sufficient to reach below the blocks.

"Once beneath the concrete the rabbits will have to remove the soil on one side only so that the mast will capsize. If all goes well the mast will become unstable and fall to the ground.

"Notification of the correct procedure will then have to be transmitted to other groups in the country so they can employ similar techniques. If the operation goes wrong then the mistakes made here will have to be intimated to the other groups so that they can learn from them and adapt accordingly for when they commence."

"My army will not make mistakes!" shouted *The Bruce*. "They will lose their heads if they do."

"I am sure you are right," said Old George.

"I wouldn't like to be in his army," cried 605.

"Ssssh!" whispered 700. "He may hear you."

"Well, it's true. He might be nice but he is very strict."

"Going off him?" whispered Sparrow.

"Oh shut up, you silly twerp!" said 605.

The Bruce stood up in front of his assembled troops. "Bring the army to attention, Burly!" he shouted.

Burly smartly came to attention himself. "Sir!" he bellowed in obedience, before taking a deep breath ready for the next shout. "Army!"

Some of the rabbits ate grass, some had dozed off but some came to the *at ease* position ready for the next order.

"Brace up! Brace up, army! 'shun!" bellowed Burly.

They all moved this time and snapped to attention. Burly turned to The Bruce. "Army ready, sir!" barked the perspiring second-in-command.

The Bruce repeated Old George's plan to the army of rabbits and told them to get to it. He told Burly to take charge and to see that a good job was done.

"Sir!" shouted Burly, turning to the army. "Move to the left, left turn! Hop in single fire, first rank, by the left. Quick, hop!"

The first rank moved off and as soon as the last rabbit of that rank cleared the assembled army, Burly shouted for the next to move out in the same fashion.

Eventually, the entire army was on the move.

Hop, hop, hop they went in a long column stretching off in to the skyline away from George and the rest of the observers. It was a most impressive sight.

"Well, that task is as well as done," said *The Bruce*. "They'll do a good job, have no fear. Now, how would you like to attend a beauty contest tonight?"

The Bruce turned to Old George and his colleagues-in-crime.

"Oh, that would be nice for a change," replied Old George. "We haven't had any social life since we left England. It will make a pleasant break."

"Good, that's settled," said *The Bruce*. "I am the senior judge at this annual event, which is the 'Miss Rabbit of the Year' finals. We usually have pipers playing and a Highland dance team. All good Scottish stuff, with haggis to finish."

Chapter 30
The Beauty Contest at Kirk O'Shotts Aerial

McAmmid Alley

After dark that evening Old George and his colleagues congregated at a disused pit shale tip. The mound rose high on three sounds like a large amphitheatre. It was an ideal private site for a beauty contest! Four Scottish wagtails had formed a dance group and were doing a sword dance over pairs of scissors which had been opened at right angles.

"Could you do that, Wagtail?" asked Old George.

"Oh, no," said Wagtail. "I'd lose my feet if I tried that."

"We'd have to fit you with skis," said Sparrow with a cheeky grin. "And an arrester hook," added Owl.

"Now come on, don't get too excited you lot," said George.

The scissor dancers finished their dance, which had been performed to the strains of a special type of bagpipe. The pipes had been made out of a scooter's inner- tube, three ballpoint pens and a piece of gas pipe. The piper himself was a large pheasant who had been specially flown in from the Queen Mother's home at Glamis Castle. He was indeed a royal piper of immense talent and dimensions.

The pipes were played by placing the piece of inner-tube around the body with the valve in the beak, the constant supply of air governed by pressure applied to the tube from one or both wings. The three pens were stuck in to the tube and lay over the port wing and shoulder, while the gas pipe led from the inner tube down to the ground. At the point of contact with the ground the tube was bent at right angles. The piece of pipe thus touching the ground contained several holes and the correct tones were produced by the royal pheasant placing his right foot over the appropriate holes for each note.

With this arrangement it was not possible for the pheasant to play and march at the same time, though a local rabbit told George that the Queen Mother was sympathetic to the pheasant's problem and consequently didn't expect him to play on-the-move – unless accompanied by an assistant.

The audience of non-army rabbits applauded the dancers, who then left the stage. Two pheasants, including the piper, then played *Amazing Grace* to the delight of the crowd.

"Aren't they good!" exclaimed Owl. "Oh, very talented," replied 700.

"I see you are enjoying the show," said *The Bruce* as he looked at Owl. "Oh yes, sir. I am very glad I came.

The Bruce nodded in acknowledgement. "After this it will be the beauty contest proper. Bring me a fresh glass of carrot juice!" His bellow was aimed at a servile rabbit who was waiting nearby.

"And for your friends, your liege?" asked the servant.

"Yes, of course. Why not. Let us all have a glass of carrot juice!" The juice duly arrived and they all indulged.

"I hope there's no salt in this," said Old George to Owl, quietly. "What was that?" asked the bird.

"Oh, nothing," replied George, remembering the fiasco over the porridge. At that moment the pipes struck up again and the announcer came on. "Who is he?" asked Old George.

"A very famous rabbit personality," replied *The Bruce*. "A rabbit by the name of McAmmid Alley."

"He's the most," cried 605.

"He sure is," said 700.

"What a glistening black coat he has," said Wagtail.

"He's our world champ. A great boxer!" said *The Bruce*. "He used to be my personal bodyguard at one time."

"Is that right?" wondered Wagtail with astonishment.

"Yes, that's really true my friend. As sure as I am standing here."

McAmmid Alley began to speak. "Howdy folks, this is the greatest here again.

I'm sure you are all glad that you came along to see me tonight."

"He likes himself," said Wagtail, looking at Owl.

"Sure does," replied Owl.

"And the beautiful young does, of course," continued McAmmid Alley. "We have some star-studded beauts for you here tonight, so without much more ado let's have them on the stage."

The competitors suddenly appeared from their burrows and paraded in front of the crowd.

"Thank you, does, that's mighty fine. You're almost as good looking as me!

Now then, folks, we'll have them back one at a time dressed in the latest creations from all over Scotland."

The stage slowly cleared and McAmmid was left standing alone. "Could I now have Miss Argyll?" he requested.

Miss Argyll came on. There was a loud shout from the crowd, with the loudest shouts of all coming from the randier bucks.

A doe announcer attempted to describe the style of dress. "Miss Argyll is wearing a summer creation of lettuce leaves threaded with asparagus. Her wide brimmed hat is an artistic-coloured net of synthetic fibre."

"You mean an old onion sack!" shouted an intoxicated buck in the front row. "Have that hooligan removed!" boomed *The Bruce*. Within seconds the hooligan had been removed and the show continued without further incident. Unfazed, Miss Argyll paraded back and forth, twirled around and walked off.

"And next we have Miss Lothian!"

Miss Lothian proved to be a buxom rabbit with big hips. Her eye lashes were at least an inch long and her ears were held together with a gold-painted bulldog clip, the like kind used to hold sheets of paper. Around her neck she wore an old wristlet watch with a shiny expanding bracelet.

Miss Perthshire

"What's that, a neck time?" asked Sparrow.

"Ssssh!" cried 605, frightened that *The Bruce* might get annoyed. Around her waist she had a string of Polo Mints.

"Would like to lick around that!" smiled 700. "Really!" scolded 605. "You are vulgar sometimes." 700 just blushed.

Her outfit was finished off by the final addition of a pair of high length boots made out of the fingers of an old glove.

"Isn't she beautiful?" mused McAmmid Alley as she made her final pirouette before leaving. There was no audible response from the audience to suggest that they agreed so he proceeded to repeat himself.

"Isn't she beautiful, you ignorant bums!" he shouted. The audience rolled up with laughter.

"Thank you kindly," said McAmmid before continuing. "And now, from the capital country, Miss Lothian!"

The audience were quick to notice the error in repeating the name. Miss Lothian was, after all, probably back in the dressing room crying her eyes out. With one accord the crowd shouted, "You've made a mistake, you ignorant bum!"

Even *The Bruce* had to laugh at the speed with which the audience reacted to McAmmid Alley's error.

"No, it's err, it's Miss Perthshire," corrected the presenter. "Are you sure now?" shouted a comedian on the back row.

Miss Perthshire made her entrance with regality until she tripped over McAmmid's big feet. "Silly sod!" she whispered to him with a smile.

Not being put off, Miss Perthshire worked her way around the floor, showing off what little she had to best advantage. It was obvious to all that she originated from an agricultural region. On her head she wore a rather large turnip top with two holes for her ears to stick through. Her bra was made out of two flip-tops from squeegee bottles and her skirt from some excess canvas, scraps leftover from the manufacturer of primitive aircraft. It had a bright silver sheen.

"Obviously been to the Strathallan Aircraft Museum," muttered *The Bruce* on seeing her feet and legs covered with cut-down wind socks.

Old George had every reason to believe the deduction. He leaned over to the observant rabbit beside him and whispered, "A bit of fly-by-night, I reckon."

"Very good, very good," chuckled *The Bruce*.

"And now, from just down the road, Miss Dunbartonshire," announced McAmmid Alley.

"This should be a hoot," said Sparrow.

Starling looked at Sparrow and nodded. "You're not kidding, she is also Miss Glasgow."

Everyone went quiet as the next doe came on the scene. She hopped on, as if she was trying to catch a number twenty-seven to the Broomielaw.

"I think her father was a ploughman," said Starling.

Round her waist she wore a belt of human hair strung with razor blades. Her ears were pierced with sharpened tacks. Her bra had two reversed mapping pins fixed in to position so that any romantic embrace would surely have given rise to instant death.

"Don't fancy her," cried 700.

The brassy piece hopped around McAmmid Alley as if she was about to attack.

Even he was a little on edge.

Suddenly, a rather dirty, mud-covered buck came charging up to *The Bruce.*

"Quick sir! The mast! There has been an accident at the mast."

"Explain yourself!"

"The mast has sunk and trapped about thirty of your army. The TV mast, sir!"

"Very well!" shouted *The Bruce.* "I'll be right along!"

"You'll need help," said Old George. "I'll get a spade and come along."

"Good, I can't risk any more of my rabbit colleagues being trapped. You should find some old tools over there; they've been lying untouched for a long time."

Old George searched for the spade near to where he'd been directed. Sure enough, he found the implement – which was actually in very good condition.

"Let's go!" he said.

The Bruce and George left the rest to enjoy the beauty contest. There was little sense in causing undue panic at this stage. On arrival at the TV mast they found the untrapped rabbits trying to dig their way beneath the subsided concrete.

"My God, they soon got beneath the concrete," exclaimed George.

"Oh yes," said Burly. "They had formed a big hole underneath but the concrete and the mast slipped before they could get out. The mast is already to fall over, we must get them out!"

Old George started to dig down as quickly as he could. "They will only need a small hole to get out," said Burly.

It must have been after about an hour of digging that George finally felt that he was getting anywhere. Suddenly, his spade went through in to nothing – he was through to the air gap beneath the concrete. He kneeled down beside the hole and shouted, "Anyone alive?"

They all waited for a reply. There was a deathly silence. "Get us out of here!" came a distant voice.

"That's them!" shouted *The Bruce* with pride. "I knew they would survive that!"

Old George stuck his hand down the hole. About six inches in was another mound of soil. He removed this with his hand and suddenly his fingers touched something warm and furry. It was a rabbit's nose!

"Attishoo! Attishoo!" came the noise from the nose as it found itself tickled.

Seconds later a rabbit pushed its way out, followed by another and then another.

The escapees were all covered in mud and dust. "Gee, thanks very much. That was a near thing."

"That's all right," said Old George. "I am really the one responsible, it is all my fault."

"No, it isn't!" retorted *The Bruce*. "I allowed my army to participate, so I am the one who's responsible."

"Look, we had better get out of here before we are found out," said Old George. "I think the mast will fall tonight without any further help from us. I can feel a breeze picking up!"

"Right, let's go!" ordered *The Bruce*.

Back at the pit bing, the beauty contest was over. The other judges had made their decision and it was unanimous:

Miss Fife was the winner. As a token of fairness, *The Bruce* decided to abstain from offering his opinion.

The crowning ceremony was duly performed by the king of the rabbits and everyone finished the evening off with carrot wine, fresh lettuce and haggis.

"Did you enjoy yourself, George?" asked *The Bruce* of his human companion. "Very much, apart from the emergency and the heavy manual work at least. It takes a toll on my old heart."

"I do hope you haven't overdone things. You have a long journey back, and presumably a lot of excitement to deal with as well."

"I am rather worried about things," said Old George. "If you could liaise with the wild cats, eagles and everyone else in Scotland I would be able to go back with a clearer mind. I really feel that I should not stay any longer."

"You have done well," said *The Bruce* in a reassuring tone. "Rest up tonight and start back tomorrow with first light. With a bit of luck the TV mast will fall down before you go!"

"I hope so, but let's first sort out what went wrong during today's mining exercise. We were lucky to avoid disaster. If we can prevent it happening to other groups of rabbits as they carry out their work, we can avoid disaster."

"Burly! Over here!" ordered *The Bruce*.

The obedient Burly duly hopped over. "Yes, sir! How can I be of help?"

"Yes, Burly. About the accident. Any ideas as to how we can avoid a recurrence?"

"We need blocks of wood to shore up the concrete as we remove the earth. Even if the wood lasts a long time it will eventually rot and cause the cement to collapse."

"You could set fire to the wood once the hole has been dug," offered George. "Good, well, as long as you know what to do, we can tell the rest. Back to your post!"

"Sir!" barked Burly, snapping to attention before leaving.

From where Owl was perched, he could see the top of the TV mast. "I'm sure that thing has moved off the vertical in the last few minutes!" he cried with enthusiasm.

"Where, where?" cried Starling, who flew up beside Owl to get a look.

Everyone turned to face the general direction of the mast, though those on the ground couldn't see a thing.

"Oh, do tell us!" cried 605. "What's happening?"

"The mast is on the move, I'm sure of it! It's going to fall," shouted Owl. "Let's get a better view!"

Every creature present hopped, ran, flew or staggered towards a high vantage point that overlooked the mast. Even while they were adjusting their seating positions the mast was moving. It was inching its way towards the ground, slowly at first and then with increasing rapidity as its guy cables began to shear and get torn free.

At forty-five degrees the mast's momentum was high and within seconds the entire structure collapsed all the way to the ground. Oddly enough, there was not a lot of noise. The ground was rather soft and covered in grass. The lack of any great noise pleased Old George no end, as he felt he would be unable to stand any more immediate hullabaloo! He just wanted to quietly walk away from the sight without fear of detection.

The Bruce must have read Old George's mind. "Let's go," he said. "As soon as the programmes cease to be transmitted there will be one hell of a stink around here. You can take refuge in the old mine buildings until tomorrow."

"Then, I must go south," said Old George, feeling a severe pain in his chest. "I really have had too much excitement."

Chapter 31
Knighted, Then Stopped by the Police

The next morning Old George woke feeling slightly better. "Come on, you lot.

We'll have to get on our way."

Everyone stirred, some eagerly and others reluctantly. They all shook hands and said their goodbyes. McAmmid Alley shadow-boxed with 605 playfully before giving her a big hug and a kiss.

"Oh, you are nice!" she smiled.

"Ma'am," he said. "If you are ever around these parts again, you see and look me up. I'd really appreciate that."

"I will, I will!" cried 605 in an excited tone.

The Bruce arrived on the scene to say farewell.

"Proud to have met you, Bruce," said Old George. Out of the corner of his eye he could see the king's army collecting. They began to close in to such an extent that Old George began to feel quite anxious. He began to wonder what was about to happen. Surely, he hadn't offended *The Bruce*? George started to panic and wish that he had the strength to run a mile as fast as possible.

"I would like to show my gratitude to you," bellow *The Bruce*, at the same time beckoning to Burly.

In his left hand, Old George could see a small wreath made from rhododendron leaves. At least, it looked like a wreath. Or was it a crown?

"Kneel down, old man," ordered *The Bruce*.

Old George thought that he had better obey and duly knelt down. *The Bruce* then produced an old kitchen knife and placed the blade first on George's right shoulder and then on his left.

"I now pronounce you, Sir George Of Shotts."

"You've been knighted!" shouted Owl. "Surprise, surprise! Old George has been knighted!"

"Three cheers for Sir George!" cried Burly.

"Hurrah! Hurrah! Hurrah!" bellowed everyone with delight. "Arise, Sir George!" ordered *The Bruce*.

Old George got up off the wet grass, brushed his trousers and stood facing the king. "I thank you, sir, for this great honour which you have bestowed upon me. I am indeed deeply touched."

"Go your way, Sir George," said *The Bruce*. "And God be with you."

"I thank you, sir," said the old man again.

With tears in his tired old eyes, Sir George and his colleagues made their way back to the car. After a little bit of bother, the engine fired up in the damp air.

"Goodbye!" they all shouted as the little vehicle moved away.

The Bruce and his followers continued to wave until the car had disappeared over the hill. It was difficult to say who was the most disappointed.

Back on the M8, the occupants sat with their thoughts. Old George still cried at the honourable tribute paid to him. He had never had anything so grand. He thought about the number of years that he had spent serving fellow man without much recognition except the present of the car from the doctor. It was a strange world, a very strange world.

The little car soon arrived at the turn-off for the road bridge. "I think we'll stay away from there just now," said Sir George. "Let's just keep driving and get clear of Edinburgh. We will return on the same road that brought us here. It will be less worry for me and my sense of direction if I can recognise landmarks."

"Very good," nodded Owl.

"That is very sensible," said 605. Still dreaming about the handsome Scottish rabbits.

At that moment, someone coughed in the back of the car.

"Erm, I don't feel like going all the way to England," said a faint voice. It was Starling, dropping a hint that he should be allowed out.

"Oh dear! I had forgotten all about you," said Sir George, apologetically. "Head in the clouds, eh!" cried Starling.

"Yes, yes. Too true," agreed the old man. "Gone to my head, it has."

Sir George pulled the Wolseley over to the side of the road and lowered the window. "Carry on with your good work," said the Old Man.

"Will do," replied Starling. "Best of luck to you all." Whereupon he flew off to rejoin his squadron.

"Oh, what a sad day of goodbyes we are having," cried 700.

"I almost wish we had never come," said Wagtail. "I really don't like saying goodbye."

"Does it stick in your craw?" said Sparrow in light-hearted tone, trying to raise everyone's feelings.

"Aye, it does that," replied 700, chuckling to himself.

The travellers eventually ended up in Princes Street. The straightness of the road reminded Owl of the canals in Northampton, Buckinghamshire and the surrounding areas.

"Are there any canals in Scotland?" he asked.

"Well of course," replied Old Sir George. "There is the Caledonian Canal and the Forth and Clyde Canal. And the Union Canal, which is quite close to here actually."

"Oh? What do they use the Union Canal for?" wondered Owl. "Making beer!" retorted George.

"Making beer? You're joking!" laughed Owl. "How can they make beer out of a canal?"

"They use the water to make the brew," said George.

"Hmm, I see," said Owl, cautiously. "I'll need to check up on that answer."

"True," said the old man. "That's why the Edinburgh beer is so good. The Japanese don't know the secret and neither do the English!"

Sir George navigated his way out of the city and out on to the open road again. The car seemed to be running quite rough but the old man put it down to the slow drive through Edinburgh. They were climbing a hill near Pathhead when Sparrow looked out of the rear window.

"Oooh, it's foggy over there," said the feathered friend.

"Where?" asked Owl, looking out of the same window. "Crikey, you're not wrong!"

Sir George took an extra-long look out of the rear window. "That's not fog, that's smoke. I do believe *we* are the cause!"

"You mean that we are on fire?" asked 700.

"'fraid so," replied Owl glumly.

George pulled the car off the road and got out to investigate the cause of the smoke. He went to the rear only to see dense blue smoke streaming from the back nearside wheel.

"Oh dear, is it serious?" shouted Wagtail from the cabin.

"I'll need to bend down to have a look," came the old man's reply.

Old George bent down so that he could see the underneath of the car and the parts around the rear brake hub.

"I think the brakes have seized," he said with some annoyance. "We will have to wait until it cools down. May take some time, so you others go and look for food if you like."

The others didn't need to be told twice to go for food. They scampered or fluttered on to the grass bank. Owl soon came back. "I can't find what I want in the day time. Waste of time, looking. I'll just make myself comfortable in the car."

After some time, George was able to touch the brake drum without burning himself. He took and old spanner and loosened the adjusting nut at the rear of the brake drum, then checked the level of brake fluid in the reservoir and, satisfied that he had enough fluid, he got ready for moving off again.

"That should do the trick!" he called. "Come on, everyone. We can get going again!"

The car soon filled up and away they went once more.

About an hour later, Sparrow reminded George that they had not heard the news for quite some time.

"Well, I was really waiting for some positive development," said George. "Oh, do pull in to a lay-by!" cried 700.

"OK," replied the old man. "I'll do that.

A lay-by soon appeared in the distance and Old George began to pull in when he suddenly noticed a fluorescent band on the side of a distant car following behind. He swerved out of the line that he was on and back on to the main road as if he had never intended to stop. 700 and 605 both fell on to the floor of the car.

"Crumbs, go steady!" bellowed 700 angrily.

"Sorry about that, buns, but there is a police car coming up in the mirror." Everyone blanched except 700, who was still nursing his bruises.

"Oh dear, do you think they are on to us?" asked Owl.

"Would be at all surprised," said Sparrow. "We may have been spotted at the bridge, or the TV mast."

"Now, now. It may just be coincidence," said Sir George. "We will just take it steady and hope that they pass us."

By this time the police vehicle was right behind the saboteurs. The car followed them for mile upon mile. Everyone began to get very nervous indeed.

"Look," said Wagtail. "This is driving me up the wall. The suspense is killing me!"

"I quite agree," said 700. "Let's pull in to the side."

George didn't know what to do. They were up hill and down dale but still the police car kept close behind. Suddenly and for no obvious reason the police car pulled out and sped off ahead of the old Wolseley. It sped over the horizon like a scalded cat and disappeared as quickly as it had arrived. They all breathed a great sigh of relief.

"Oh, thank God!" said Sparrow. "I couldn't have taken much more of that. The suspense was too much!" The little bird proceeded to faint on the seat.

"Open the window, George, and let in some air," shouted Owl.

Sir George as he was bid and the car filled with nice clean fresh air. Sparrow began to flutter and cough.

"There we are old son, feeling better?" asked 700.

"Yes, thanks," said a rather weary-looking Sparrow. "I'll be OK in a second."

"I don't know about that," retorted George as he came over the brow of a hill and spotted something ahead. "The police are up there in the next lay-by!" Everyone looked ahead with horror.

"Oh crikey, no! Not again!" cried Wagtail. "This must be the end!"

A large copper was seen to get out of the white police car. He stood at the side of the road facing the oncoming Wolseley, his left hand outstretched.

"What's he doing? Testing for rain?" asked Sparrow in an effort to break the agonisingly tense atmosphere.

It was quite obvious that the law-man wanted them to pull in, so Old George slowed down and tucked in to the lay-by behind the big Ford. The copper strode across to the driver's window of the old car.

"Good day, sir. Sorry to bother you but we were admiring your car back there. What a good runner she is! Fancy flying up those hills like that. Really great stuff! I hope my heart is in such good condition when I am here age."

Old Sir George laughed with relief. "Yes, she is still very strong and has, in fact, always been that way!"

"Only one thing though, sir," said the constable. "Your off-side rear wheel is quite badly buckled. I would advise that you change it."

"Oh thank you, constable. I will do that now. Thank you very much for telling me. I don't feel too well but I must think of road safety, mustn't I?"

The constable looked at Old George. "I'll give you a hand, old son," he said. At this point he shouted to the other constable, who was still sitting in the police car. "Willie, give us a hand over here!"

Willie duly appeared and began to help the constable to change the spare wheel, which was positioned on the rear of the car. It only took the two strong men a few minutes to sort out. George was quietly impressed.

"There we are, old son," said the satisfied constable. "Best wishes to you and keep her going!"

"Thank you kindly," said Old George, feeling so guilty that he felt like confessing to all his crimes. *Perhaps this is the new police psychology?* he thought to himself. *Play on the villain's conscience!*

Chapter 32
The Final Stage Home

The police car left in a cloud of dust, leaving the saboteurs alone again. George looked round. He was certainly *all* alone. Where were the rest of his colleagues?

Old George called, "Come on you lot, it's all clear!"

Suddenly, the old man heard a scuffling noise beneath the front seats. He looked down and out popped Owl, then 700, followed by 605, Wagtail and Sparrow.

"God, that was close," said Owl in a sweat. "That was much too close for comfort."

"Cowards!" shouted George. "You deserted me in my hour of danger."

"Did we really?" said Sparrow. "Sorry about that but we knew that they would ask awkward questions if they saw us. Even now, they are bound to remember you and the car if any witnesses to our deeds come forward."

"You are quite right," sighed George. "Actually, I am quite glad you vanished from view. I am sure it would have ruined everything otherwise."

"So, *now* can we listen to the radio?" asked Owl.

"Yes, I think the time is right for that. Let us have a rest and listen before progressing further with our journey!" replied the old man.

Old George got the radio on to his lap and switched it on. Nothing happened, so he twiddled the tuning knob back and forth hoping to pick up the evasive stations.

"Oh, give it a bang!" uttered Owl in a fit of impatience.

"Now, be patient," said George in a fatherly tone. "Don't be in such a rush.

Rome wasn't built in a day, you know."

Owl fluffed up his feathers in defensive annoyance, mumbling under his breath. Sparrow mumbled away in unison, comically imitating Owl's utterances.

"I'll batter you," said Owl, getting really angry.

"Now now, you two. Pack it in. We are all on the same side, or have you forgotten?" said George.

Owl and Sparrow apologised to each other.

"Give it a dunt!" said Owl, encouraging George to wallop the radio.

"You apologise in one breath and then continue to be impatient," scorned the old man. "It is a good job that we are going home. We are all getting edgy."

"You can say that again," said Wagtail. "It's a bit much for me."

Old Sir George fiddled for a few moments longer and then gave the radio a gentle knock against his knee. He then moved the tuner up and down the scale yet again. The thing blurted in to life suddenly, first in German and then French as the various wavelengths were interrupted. Eventually he managed to get a faint signal in the English language but he could only just pick out the speech. It appeared to be the termination of a classical recital of some sort.

"I've got something," he shouted, holding the receiver against his ear. "Oh, that's good," said 605.

"Sssh, I think there is going to be an announcement!"

"We apologise to all listeners to English programmes. A number of transmissions are being sent out on reduced power due to an emergency situation. We must remind you that all transmissions may have to stop within the hour. We will endeavour to maintain hourly news bulletins. TV programmes are also affected in the region of Central Scotland. The time is twelve noon. Here is the news for today."

"Everybody! Here is the news!" whispered George.

The radio voice went on. "Late last night the Kirk O'Shotts aerial mast fell to the ground under mysterious circumstances. At first it was thought to have been caused by subsidence brought about by recent heavy rain in the area.

Investigations by the police and the BBC have found of extreme and unusual activity in the region of ground at the base of the mast. Marks in the soil indicated that a spade had been used to excavate part of the foundations. A police spokesman said that a large gang had obviously been active. The reason for the sabotage is not known but it is thought that it was a deliberate attempt to disrupt TV transmissions in the very densely populated Central Belt of Scotland.

"The sabotage at Kirk O'Shotts may be connected with the destruction of the Forth Road Bridge. The destruction of the bridge has led to a partial paralysis of industry in the area. Most drivers have cooperated with demands to stay off the roads in West Lothian and Fife if a journey between the two counties is planned.

"A top-level meeting is in progress at the moment between town councillors, MPs, the armed forces and the police. The sole purpose of the meeting is to discuss the possibility of providing a ferry service for industry and the working public. This means that there could be a return to the situation that existed in the early sixties, when four ferry boats were in operation on the South to North Queensferry passage.

"Efforts to establish an emergency ferry link are being hampered by the need to remove the marina at North Queensferry pier. The problem of finding suitable boats will likely be left to the armed forces, though boats with shallow drafts will have to be used as the water and both piers has silted up considerably since the departure of the old ferries. A spokesman at Rosyth dockyard stated that dredging would have to be undertaken prior to any large ferry boat being introduced.

"Today, we have Admiral Blenkinsop-Hardlie-Nelson in the studio to discuss the situation as seen from the naval side. Now then, Admiral Blenkinsop-Hardlie-Nelson, first of all do you mind me calling you Admiral Nelson?"

"Rather you call me Admiral Blenkinsop-Hardlie-Nelson, actually. *The Admiralty* may get upset of you call me Nelson, while to use the title *Hardlie-Nelson* may be misinterpreted by your public to mean that my professional standing in the

Royal Navy – the senior force despite what some may think – is err, to say the least, suspect. No, I'm sorry old boy, it'll have to be the whole thing or nothing at all. Now, about the questions that you were about to ask me."

"Well thank you very much, Admiral Blenkinsop-Hardlie-Nelson. I'm afraid that's all we have time for today. And now, for the foreign news. In South Africa the…" Old George switched off the radio.

"Well, that was one for the book," said Owl. "The old admiral didn't get a chance to fly his flag, did he?"

"Balls are too heavy!" said Sparrow with a grin. "I beg your pardon?" said 605.

"Balls too heavy!" repeated Sparrow at the top of his voice. "Really, Sparrow, you want to wash your mouth out."

"W-E-L-L it's true. Some 'ave 'em and some don't," said Sparrow in explanation.

"What do you mean?" bellowed 605 in a scolding tone. "Don't you try to get out of it!"

Old Sir George thought that he had better come to Sparrow's rescue. "I think he is referring to the naval custom of placing red discs on flags of St George's cross. The number of discs or balls denotes the seniority of the admiral or commodore. Two balls denotes a rear admiral, one ball a vice admiral and none, an admiral. A second-class commodore is allowed one ball on his pennant."

"You would think a vice admiral would need all the balls that he could get his hands on," chuckled Sparrow.

"Now, now, now, that's quite sufficient chat from you, me lad," retorted Old George. "Anyway, we had better go. If we hurry, we can get home by early evening."

The little car sped on its way on to the A697 through Greenlaw and Coldstream, as before, then on to Crookham and Wooler. Eventually arriving at the new by-pass for Morpeth and Newcastle.

"Oh, here's that smoky old tunnel again!" said Wagtail unhappily. "I feel sick already, let me out!"

Old George paid the fee and drove as quickly as possible underneath the River Tyne. As they came out of the tunnel the thick blue air gave way to a bright afternoon. Soon they were on the A1 again heading south, past the army base at Catterick, although there was nothing to be seen from the roadside.

"Is that an airfield?" asked Wagtail.

Old George looked to his left to see the runways and hangars.

"Oh yes, there are a number of airfields around here," he said. "They were used during the war to protect the industrial midlands. For example, there is Rufforth and Dishforth and Linton-on-Ouse, from where the Halifax bombers used to fly. Linton was used by the Fleet Air Arm at one time for pilot training, too. Used to fly prop and jet Provosts and Vampires among others. Run by the RAF, though."

"Not Vampire bats?" asked Sparrow with a look of surprise. "No, silly! Vampire jet aircraft," said Old George.

"Oh, what a relief. I was just about to hide," replied the little bird.

At the next filling station George pulled in and bought petrol and sandwiches.

The lady in the tea room looked annoyed. "Hard day?" asked George in sympathy.

"Damn television's been playing up all day. Now it's gone off completely." she replied.

"Any idea what's wrong?" wondered the old man.

"Somebody said it had to do with the transmitters. Been saboteurs in Scotland, so they say. S'pose it's the terrorists or something," she said.

"Yes, probably," said George. "Well, best be off. Many thanks."

Old George climbed back in to the car. "It's happening down here as well," he said. "They are having TV trouble."

"Oh, crikey! They might have waited for us to get on and off the M1!" cried Wagtail.

"Let's get out of here quick-like," said 605.

George quickly wolfed down his sandwiches, started the car and drove off.

The journey down the M1 was long and boring this time. The weather was nice and bright but they all wanted to get settled in at the cottage. The journey was made longer by Old George's tiredness. He didn't seem to have the same amount of energy as before. He thought the fumes from the traffic may be the cause, plus the change in air and the excitement, of the journey to Scotland.

They jogged along in the slow lane, only occasionally overtaking a lorry. At junction 16 George pulled off on to the A45 and then left on to the A5. They were almost home and dry!

"Soon be there, now," said the Old Man. There was no reply. The animals and birds were fast asleep. George took out his handkerchief from his right-hand pocket and wiped his forehead and blood-shot eyes. He looked in the interior mirror for a brief second to see what his eyes looked like. They felt very sore and tired. Through the blurred vision he could see that his right eye in particular was very blood-shot. The muscles above his eyebrows were very taut and he had a headache.

Oh, for a good meal and a rest, he thought.

A few miles further on he swung up to the cottage. "We are here!" he called. "Come on, you lazy-bones!"

He gave 700 and 605 a nudge before getting out of the car.

"Oh, err, what? Where are we?" asked several voices in the bleary-eyed crew. "At the cottage!" replied Old George with a beaming smile.

"Oh, yippee!" came a cry in unison.

The noise must have roused the inmates of the cottage, for they all ran out to welcome the old man and adventurers.

"Welcome back," said Big Puss. "Had a good time, George?"

"Sir George, to you!" said Owl with pride.

Big Puss thought Owl was being sarcastic. "You're not very friendly," he said. "You don't understand," said Owl. "George has been knighted for his work in Scotland."

"But the Queen isn't in Scotland," replied Big Puss, confused.

"You do not require the Queen."

"Then he hasn't been knighted!" moaned the big cat.

"Oh yes he has!" said 700 in defence. "By King Rabbit The Bruce, nonetheless."

"King Rabbit The Bruce? Who is he?" asked Fox, now completely recovered from his injuries.

"The king rabbit of Scotland," said Old George. "Now let's change the subject and get some tea!"

"OK, Sir George," said Big Puss, realising he had been defeated.

Old George didn't much like the idea of being called *Sir* George in his own little cottage. Somehow it seemed out of place. *I suppose I'll have to get used to it,* he thought.

"So how are you, Fox? How are you getting on? You look fit enough now," asked George.

Fox felt a bit guilty for being found at the cottage. "Oh, I am fine," he said. "But I thought I would be better off staying here a little longer so that I could see you. We were all very worried about you when you were in Scotland. We only received a few scant messages about you from passing birds."

"Yes, it was all very secret stuff. I am sorry you were all left wanting."

"Oh, that's all right," said Fox. "Glad to see you back, although you look very tired."

"Yes, I *am* very tired. Very tired indeed."

During the evening Old George related their adventures to the other animals and then retired to bed early. The car was left outside the cottage for the night because Old George intended to buy food the following day. He reckoned that another night out of a garage wouldn't do the old girl any harm.

Chapter 33
Phantom in the Night

George and his war cabinet slept soundly despite their deep worries about arrest.

Downstairs, Owl quietly dozed on the mantelpiece of the fireplace. The clock struck two o' clock, then quarter to three. Outside, everything was deadly quiet except for the sound of a distant fox calling its mate. Close by, a car starter began to churn away. It was such a smooth, gentle type of noise; blunted by the hedges and trees. Nobody stirred. The noise went on and on and on until eventually the engine and starter ran together. At that moment the engine began to run under its own power and the starter motor switched off. As time went by, the engine began to run more smoothly and settled back to a gentle burble. Still, nobody stirred.

After about half an hour, Owl's very sensitive lungs began to expand more deeply. He was beginning to feel distressed even though he was still asleep. He felt that he was not getting enough air. The deterioration in his breathing made him wake up with a start. He sniffed the air. Something strange was going on. The air in the room seemed to be stale and full of fumes. It was then that he thought he heard a car engine running. "Is this my imagination?" he wondered to himself. "No! That *is* a car engine!"

Wagtail and Sparrow began to stir, followed by 700 and 605. "Oh, my head hurts," cried Sparrow. "I do have a headache!"

"Me too," exclaimed Wagtail. "I am gasping for breath."

"Something is going on," said Owl. "I am sure I can hear a car engine outside, and the fumes are coming in to the house."

"You're right!" cried 700. "We are all being gassed! I'll go up and get George." 700 bolted up the stairs to wake up the old man, who was still sound asleep. He jumped on to the bed and licked George's face.

"George, wake up! Wake up, George! Someone is trying to gas us!"

The old man woke up with a terrible start. "Eh, what? What's that? Who's there?

Get away or I'll hit you!"

"It's okay, George. It's only me, 700. You must get up; someone has started the car and the fumes are filling the house."

The old man eventually came to and gathered his thoughts together, along with his trousers and a shirt. "I locked the car and have the keys here," he said scornfully. "How can anyone start the car?"

"Oh, do hurry," cried 700. "They might take the car away."

The old man struggled to put on his clothes in a hurry but managed, then got his slippers on and beckoned to 700. "Let's go and see what all this is about," he said.

By the time a very stiff George got in to the front room the fumes were really quite bad.

"Dear, oh dear," said George, picking up an old walking stick. "I'd best go out and see what is happening."

"Do be careful!" cried the animals. "I'll come with you," said Fox.

"Me too," added Owl. "You may need help."

Old George unlocked the front door and quietly put his head outside. "Sssh, keep down and follow me," he whispered to his assistants. They crept along the path and down to the hedge, to where the car was parked. In the darkness they could see the shadowy vehicle, the lights were not on and the doors were still shut. As far as George could remember the Wolseley was still parked where he had left it. A shudder went down his spine. *What a mysterious business,* he thought. "Just what is going on?"

"I'll reconnoitre," said Owl. "Leave it to me, but you stay where you are."

Owl flew off, climbing as he went to about fifteen feet. He circled the car and flew behind all the trees and bushes in the immediate area. After a few swoops and dives he returned to report that everything was clear.

"But there must be someone about," said George, feeling a bit annoyed. "Oh alright, I'll go round again," puffed Owl, taking off once more.

Fox and George watched the shadow fly up and over the car and round the bushes. Owl disappeared for a few moments and then returned in the reverse direction before landing on George's shoulder.

"You can go to the car now, George. It is definitely all clear. There is nobody about."

Old George reluctantly agreed, gripped the walking stick he carried even harder and moved forward. He was so cautious that Fox ended up taking the lead. "Follow me," said the brave animal. "You'll be OK."

"Thanks very much," cried the old man with audible relief. "I don't feel too heroic at the moment."

The old man knelt down at the driver's door and very cautiously reached for the handle. A frog jumped over his foot, touching the unsocked skin as it went. "Cripes! What was that!?" bellowed the old man, jumping up on to his feet at the same time. His head collided with the branch of a low, overhanging tree. The impact sounded like two coconuts colliding in a chamber pot. A pigeon which had been disturbed by the noise took off from a branch immediately above George. It relieved itself as it flew off, as all birds do when they are navigating over Homo Sapiens. The unseen excrement slithered down Old George's cheek and quickly disappeared behind his thick beard. The speed of absorption was a sight to behold. Nothing so efficient had ever been produced by even the cutting-edge work of the synthetic sponge companies.

Man still has a lot to learn, thought George, wiping his face with a handkerchief.

Undeterred, the old man made a positive dive at the car door, only to find that it was still locked. The mystery deepened. There was nobody in the car and yet the engine was running.

"Have you got the keys?" asked Owl.

"Yes, I have them in my pocket," replied George, whereupon he pulled out the keys and put one of them in to the lock. The door opened easily, as it had always done. "There isn't a key in the ignition," said George, leaning over to look. "I'll put a key in to the hole and see if I can turn the engine off."

The key went in to the ignition easily enough so George turned it back and forth.

Nothing happened at first but then the engine suddenly died. All went quiet. "What a strange how-de-do," said Fox.

"Yes," replied a much-relieved old man. "But I think I know what went wrong. This car has an automatic starter which switches itself in and out until the engine fires. Obviously, the wiring has short circuited during the night, causing the starter to come in to operation. With it being summer and a nice warm engine block it would have started relatively easily."

"Oh, you are clever," said Fox.

"Not clever enough," replied Old George. "I should have realised the possibility of that happening before I got myself in to a stew. It really frightened me, it did."

"Understandable," consoled Owl.

"Well, let's get back to the cottage, have some rest and then we will get breakfast before going off to the village for our rations! The car can then go back in to the garage and out of the way. It's done its job for now."

"Just one thing," said Fox. "What if it happens again?"

"Good lad," smiled Old George. "I'll remove the battery leads before we go inside."

He began to remove the leads but decided there was no need for the others to wait and encouraged them to return inside.

"OK, but don't be too long," said Owl.

Chapter 34
George Takes Ill

George fumbled away with the spanners and cables until the job was safely done. He checked that the car was locked up and started his return journey up the path to the cottage. He had only gone a few paces when a severe pain went through his chest. It was so severe that he immediately fell to his knees. After a few seconds in this position he collapsed on to the ground. All was silent. There was nobody there to help.

Meanwhile, Fox and Owl were joking about the old car and George's fear of the mysterious situation. After about twenty minutes of laughing Owl turned to the rest and asked if they thought it would take long to uncouple a car battery.

"Wouldn't think so," replied 700. "I'd have thought Old George would be coming up the path by now."

Owl looked out of the little window on to the path. There was no sign of George. "I'm getting worried," said Wagtail. "Maybe there was someone out there after all?"

"No, I am sure there was not," replied Owl. "I don't miss anyone hiding in the dark, not with these eyes. To me it is as good as daylight."

"I'm going to go and see if he is OK," said 605, already making for the door.

"No, I'll go," interrupted Big Puss. "About time I helped."

Big Puss immediately disappeared in to the darkness. After a short time he came in to view of the car. Lying between was the dark shadow of Old George. He dashed up to the motionless body. Old George moaned and moved on to his side.

"George, George, are you all right?" asked Big Puss in a frenzy. "What's happened?"

"It's my old heart playing up," replied the old man as he struggled for breath. "Get me back to the house."

"I'll need help. I'll go and get some of the others."

Big Puss ran all the way back to the cottage. "Quick!" he shouted. "Quick! You, you and you, follow me!"

Without hesitation, the big cat, 700, 605 and Fox dashed out of the door. "What's happened?" asked the impatient Owl as he flew out along with them. "No time for questions," replied Big Puss. "Just get Old George back in to bed."

They soon arrived by the old man's side. He looked a sorry sight, just laid there like that.

"Please go easy with me," said George. "But get me away from here and in to the house."

With a bit of a struggle the old man was helped in to a semi-upright position. He places his left hand on Fox's back and the two rabbits pulled at his trouser legs.

Eventually they arrived back at the cottage.

"Thank God," said Old George. "I shouldn't have been moved but I couldn't lay there all night. I'll need to rest in the downstairs room. I daren't go upstairs, it could be fatal for me."

Old George laid himself out on the settee. "The car will just have to stay out there. I had better not drive tomorrow."

A feeling of depression hung over the cottage. Without George, everything would fall apart. He was the mainstay of *Operation Upset* and must be looked after!

"Look," said Old George. "We must get provisions today but I will not be fit to go into the village. I will write out a list and Fox will have to take it for me."

"That's a very sensible idea," said Wagtail.

"And I don't mind," said Fox, "But won't it be dangerous for me to go near the village?"

"Normally, yes, it would," said George. "But if I scribble out a line now you can take it in to the village with a basket. Leave the basket at the Post Office and the lady who runs it will get the shopping for me. The postal van can bring the full basket back to us and I can pay the driver."

"What a great idea that is!" smiled 605.

"Well, you have to think ahead when you live out here," said George. The old man reached for a pencil which laid on the table beside him. "Get me that old piece of paper from the windowsill, would you?"

Wagtail flew over to the window and, with some difficulty, managed to transport it across to the old man.

"That was a job for an owl!" said Wagtail, gasping to get air in to his lungs. "You'll have my heart running as bad as your own!"

Old George chuckled to himself. "Aye, I suppose you're right."

The old man took the pencil and began to write out the list of provisions. One pound of margarine, one pound of butter, a dozen eggs, a big bag of teabags, bacon. The list went on and on.

"Oh, and I suppose I had better get some carrots and plenty of fresh greens for everyone in case we run short. And cat food for Big Puss, of course, in case it is still unsafe for him to return to the farmyard. How about dog biscuits for you, fox?"

Oh thank you," replied Fox. "But I think that I should be leaving for you after I have delivered the basket to the Post Office."

"And I think I should be making my own way again as well," said Big Puss. "You have enough to do looking after yourself. In fact, I think most, if not all the other animals, feel that you have done enough for them and that they should start making their own lives."

"That means that I am left with the main members of the war cabinet," said George.

"Yes, that's right," said Big Puss. "There will only be Owl, Sparrow, Wagtail, 700 and 605 living here with yourself as from today. We will of course be in touch if you need us. We aren't deserting you; we're just trying to make your life easier."

"I appreciate your thoughtfulness," replied the old man. "You have all done very well. I'm sure the guinea pigs and mice will find something useful to do once they have settled elsewhere. When do you intend to leave?"

"I think we should leave with Fox and then go our separate ways," replied the big cat.

"That's fine with me," said George.

The old man finished his list of requirements and placed it in the basket which Fox had found in the kitchen. "There now, on your way while the going is good."

Big Puss rounded up the others and they all said their goodbyes. Fox jumped up and swung the door handle down. The door moved open and they all filed out.

"Best of luck to you all," said the old man with a tear in his eye. "I hope we will meet again."

Suddenly, they were no more. The place was quiet with only the war cabinet present. They all looked at each other. It felt to them all as though it was the end of an important stage in *Operation Upset.*

Chapter 35
Meanwhile at the House of Commons

Recent events had made such an impact on MPs that the Prime Minister had scheduled an open debate in the House of Commons. The Prime Minster, Mr Gupta, (the first non-white PM of Britain) opened the discussion with a summary of these mysterious events. He presented known facts of attacks against vandals, muggers, television aerial installations and the Forth Road Bridge.

Prime Minister: "And now I come to dee problem of the removal of the very fine bridge which no longer goes across the ever so fine River Forth. Oh, such a terrible tragedy for the Royal Navy to have to put to rights."

The Speaker of the House, a Mr Modha, sees the MP for Glamorgan jumping up and down in his seat.

"Do you wish to question the Prime Minister, Mr Leek?"

"Mr Speaker, thank you. I would. Can the Prime Minister give any indication when the River Forth will be free of debris?"

PM: "The Navy is moving in salvage craft as we speak but they do not expect to achieve very much without the assistance of the Dutch, and possibly American, navies. It is all a question of availability of craft sufficiently large to lift the debris. This is not a normal scenario by any means."

The PM continued: "It is expected that the construction of a replacement bridge will take at least two years, plus the time taken to remove the damaged structure of the old bridge. A total time of at least two years and three months."

The leader of the opposition, Margeurite Thatchurier, puts up her hand and is given permission to speak (it must be noted that this most honourable lady has recently changed her name by Deed Poll in order to bring herself closer to the Common Market).

M. Thatchurier: "Is there any truth in the rumour that the Labour government intends to use the two million unemployed citizens of the UK as slave-labour for the hurried construction of the new bridge?"

PM: "Oh golly me, no. I don't know from where the honourable fine lady gets these notions."

M. Thatchurier: "Thank you."

PM: "And now after that fine interruption I would like *hiccup*, *hiccup*. I would like to *hiccup*. Oh dear me, the curry was too strong this morning. I am *hiccup* most *hiccup* disturbed."

Mr Speaker: "Perhaps someone could continue for the honourable Prime Minister?"

Mr Ransack-Pillage (MP for Orkney and of Viking descent): "Perhaps I could carry on for the Prime Minister? After all, I wrote his speech."

Mr Speaker: "Thank you, Mr Ransack-Pillage. Please proceed."

The Prime Minister whispers his thanks to the honourable MP from Orkney and then proceeds to hiccup his way out of the house.

Mr Ransack-Pillage: (Starting the speech from the beginning) "This open discussion has been…"

Mr Speaker: I must point out to the honourable gentleman from Orkney that although he may well have written the Prime Minister's speech there is little to be gained by starting from the very beginning, despite the fact that the honourable member for Glossop has only just woken up from what must have been a much-needed snooze."

Mr Ransack-Pillage: "I beg your pardon, Mr Speaker. I will commence from where the honourable Prime Minister ceased."

Mr Speaker: "Thank you very much. I am sure the house will welcome your compliance with my request. Now get on with it, man. It'll soon be lunch time."

Mr Ransack-Pillage: (Clearly put out by the remarks) "Err, well, err, where was I. Ah, yes, the bridge. Well, in the meantime it will be necessary to use landing craft specially built for the purpose of ferrying vehicles across the Forth. Small craft have been put in to use already but these are far from satisfactory because of the size of modern haulage vehicles. Perhaps one month will be necessary for the establishment of a reasonable ferry service.

"In any event, immense disruption of industrial life can be expected in the north.

Special traffic arrangements will undoubtedly be necessary to ensure a smooth flow. Some of the problems will be alleviated by moving traffic on to the rail system but unfortunately recent cut-backs in the railways are going to cause problems which cannot be rectified. This tragedy with the bridge has highlighted the absurdity of earlier decisions to reduce the scope of the railways. Like the snows of winter, it does not take much to disrupt our civilised way of life."

M. Thatchurier: "Whose fault is that?"

Mr Speaker: "I do wish that the honourable lady would indicate her intention to speak before blurting out the questions. I really do object."

M. Thatchurier: "Will Mr Speaker please accept my apology?"

Mr Speaker: "Oh, I suppose so!"

Mr Ransack-Pillage looks over his half glasses towards the Speaker.

Mr Speaker: "Will the honourable gentleman please go on."

Mr Ransack-Pillage: "Thank you, sir. The use of a ferry service means the marina at the north side of the Forth will have to be removed."

Mr Billy Anti-Queen Samilton (MP for Central Fife): "May I ask a question of Mr Ransack-Pillage?"

Mr Speaker: "You may, but keep it short."

Mr Samilton: "Will the owner of the marina be compensated by the government?"

Prime Minister (from the back of the hall): "Certainly not! This is a time of national disaster. Anyway, he's a member of the Tory party."

M. Thatchurier: "I object to the Prime Minister's last remark."

Mr Speaker: "I do think, Mr Prime Minister, that your sense of humour got a little out of hand when you referred to a certain person being a member of the other side."

PM: "I am sorry, Mr Speaker."

Mr Speaker: "Do you wish to take over your speech again?"

PM: "No, thank you. Mr Ransack-Pillage is doing very well."

M. Thatchurier: "Watch your job. He'll have it off you!"

Mr Speaker: "Really, these outbursts must cease! Please go on, Mr Ransack- Pillage."

Mr Ransack-Pillage: "With regard to the proposed petrochemical complex at Mossmoran in Fife and the liquid gas terminal at Braefoot Bay, I must say that the oil companies concerned are most disturbed at the destruction of the Forth Bridge. It has been estimated that the cost of the installation will now be doubled because of the difficulties with transportation of pre-fabricated parts and castings. The vulnerability of the area to terrorist attack is now under serious question. Prior to the destruction of the bridge, terrorism was not considered to be a major hazard."

Mr Samilton: (After receiving permission to speak) "I am most concerned about employment in the affected area. If the petrochemical complex does not go forward then associated industries, like plastics, will not be developed in the area either. Surely a new bridge could be built across the Forth at a point west of the Kincardine Bridge where the river is a lot narrower?"

PM: (Stands up) "This is being looked into. There is, however, a strong lobby by local action groups – as I'm sure you know. They are concerned about: Possible explosions, the low number of jobs created, the loss of a very valuable area of scenic beauty at Braefoot Bay. These fears are very real and the Scottish Secretary is giving lengthy thought to all views and interests."

Mr Samilton: "Damned conservationists. Jobs are more important."

Mr McNulty-Campbell (MP for West Lothian): "With Mr Speaker's permission, I would like to say that there is little sense in having a job if you are likely to be blown up by the thing that you are paid to create. Furthermore, if you ruin the countryside and then give people a reduced working week as demanded by the unions where are they going to go for pleasure? We must stop this nonsense somewhere. The oil in the world is going to run out in the foreseeable future. We all have enough plastic items to do us a lifetime. Why build more factories to increase production, which will increase the disposability of plastic items, encourage waste and hence the waste of oil?"

MP for Buckinghamshire: "Here, here!"

The whole house had to agree that Mr McNulty-Campbell's point made sense.

MP for Cumberland: "It is about time that we got down to doing something about this business of constantly expanding. We owe it to future generations to leave room for them to manoeuvre. We are always saying that the country is being ruined and that things are not the way they were. Surely nobody else is responsible for that? *We* are the ones who are at fault. *We* are the decision makers. It is about time that sensible stagnation, for the want of a better word, became fashionable.

"Recent events have made us realised how vulnerable we are. Why are we always in such a rush to alter and destroy that which is good, quiet, clean and picturesque? We knock down old buildings and without consideration for the damp and dreary British weather we put up dark-coloured buildings in their place. We call this progress. Rubbish!"

Mr Speaker: "While I appreciate the honourable gentleman's remarks, I feel that he has let himself get somewhat carried away as it were." (The house roared with laughter) "I would like to add that there is little need for laughter. I would suggest, in fact, that the honourable members of the House might like to think on the honourable members' comments, however irrelevant they may be to the earlier discussion."

MP for South Oxford: "I think the honourable gentleman is right to mention the subject of brick buildings. Everything we build affects something else. The density of population in this country is such that we must think of the long-term effects of what we do. Every day we hear of some action group being set up. We are all getting on each other's nerves. We can't get away from our neighbours even if we want to."

MP for Hertfordshire: "A slight exaggeration!"

Mr Speaker: "Order, order!"

The MP for South Oxford continues: "And to be quite honest I am most pleased about the recent loss of television. I wish I lived in an area which had been affected."

(The PM is handed a piece of paper, which he reads to himself).

PM: "With the permission of Mr Speaker I must inform the honourable gentleman that he does in fact live in an area which has been affected. I have just been informed that two TV transmitters have gone out of action under mysterious circumstances."

(A hundred murmurs could be heard running through the House).

Mr Speaker: "Order, please. Order in the house!" (Three Scottish MPs continued to chat amongst themselves) "Order there! Will those honourable gentlemen please come to order! This is a very serious situation under discussion."

Mr Ransack-Pillage: "The question of TV entertainment is causing Her Majesty's Government a lot of concern. It is intended that all safety regulations in cinemas and theatres, halls and social clubs will be lifted until such time as the situation returns to normal. According to the BBC it will take three months to get each damaged aerial back in to operation. As an interim measure, Her Majesty's Government will supply film equipment to any responsible organisation on request.

"Orders have been given to all military camps and stations that their cinemas and sporting facilities should be made available to the public. Money is being made available to expedite the setting-up of sports centres and old folk's clubs."

MP for North Buckinghamshire: "What arrangements are being made for students of the Open University whose home studies depend on educational TV programmes?"

Mr Ransack-Pillage: "The Open University is providing video cassettes and are negotiating with a Japanese firm to help provide necessary equipment to play them."

MP for Suffolk: "Why are British firms not being given the orders for such equipment?"

Mr Ransack Pillage: "Apparently the electronics firms in this country cannot possibly supply equipment in a reasonable time-frame."

MP for Northampton: "I am terribly concerned about the cost of all these arrangements for education and entertainment. Would it not be cheaper to leave the public to their own resources? After all, if TV transmissions are going to return to normal within a few months then surely we have little need to worry."

Mr Ransack-Pillage: "Recent events have shown weaknesses in our way of life.

Her Majesty's Government feels that too much emphasis has been placed on TV viewing. The nation as a whole is forgetting how to communicate. The increased use of telephones is also turning us in to a faceless number of voices. Overall, this has to be seen as a retrograde step, although, where urgency is essential the aforementioned method of communication is ideal.

"We feel, however, that *everything* is now to be considered an emergency.

People want things done immediately and will not write a letter. Perhaps people should be made to slow down and take more time over what they are going to do and say."

MP for Berkshire: "More bureaucracy, you mean. Surely we have enough of that already?"

MP for North Yorkshire: "What right has the government to dictate to the nation in this manner? Surely this is an infringement of public liberty and freedom?"

Mr Ransack-Pillage: "How many people do you meet today who enjoy life? As parents, we are always being confronted by bored and fed-up children, or children who have seen more than what is good for them on the TV. With the advent of colour TV, the bloodshed and violence is so realistic that is becoming a normal way of life to them. Their senses are being dulled by this constant barrage of violence. We all know the outcome only too well.

MP for Lancashire: "I am glad that we have got around to violence, its cause and cure. The attacks, or suggested attacks, by animals on muggers and their like has surely proved a very important point to the complacent government. Is *their* effectiveness in dealing with this not proof that an 'eye for an eye' and a 'tooth for a tooth' is the correct approach? I, and many others in the House today, have advocated this approach for years but we have always been shouted down.

(Howls of derision from some corners of the house)

"And well you may jeer, gentleman, but we now have the proof that I have been after for years!"

MP for Berwick: "Is the effectiveness of the animals' actions not a case of shock and surprise, more than the savagery of the punishment?"

Mr Ransack-Pillage: "I think the honourable gentleman may well be correct."

MP for Lancashire: "I think Mr Ransack-Pillage is hedging the issue. The police often surprise villains but the crime still goes on. I am convinced that it is the physical damage caused by the animals and the fact that the villains are being confronted by a superior force. In many cases these cowards have only had to overcome an old-age pensioner to get what they want. They have become accustomed to winning and up until recently they knew that physical violence would never be used against them. They were always the ones to hand it out at random. This has now changed! The shoe is on the other foot. Surely Her Majesty's Government is not going to ignore the massive reduction in crime over the last few days?"

(The House shouts "Here, here!" in agreement).

"I personally am not concerned about *why* the animals are behaving in this amazing way or who trained them. Perhaps I should be concerned, but quite frankly as long as it goes on in this very satisfactory manner, I will do nothing to stop it."

(A great many more cries of "Here, here!" came bellowing from his supporters).

MP for Perth and Kinross: "The honourable gentleman from Lancashire touched on one very important point just now, although I must add that I am not suggesting for one moment that the other points he raised were not important, but I am very interested in *who* trained the animals to behave in such a manner. Nobody here today has shed any light on the subject. The mystery does not help Her Majesty's Government because many of my constituents feel that it is all part of a top-secret government plan.

"My constituents are also thinking in terms of secret drugs being used by government research establishments. To understand this train of thought we must turn our minds back to the initial outbreaks of myxomatosis in the Fifties. Many people in this country feel that the virus was deliberately introduced by the government. Can you, sir, enlighten us any further?"

Mr Ransack-Pillage: "I am afraid that I cannot comment on this point. The government are as much in the dark over this subject of animal behaviour as is the honourable member from Kinross. Police investigations are being conducted around the clock in order to find an answer. Her Majesty's Government is, of course, in touch with police progress and certain information has come to light which should help in the early settlement of the Forth Road Bridge mystery. I am afraid that I can say no more about this subject of crime-detection."

And so the debate went on in to the late afternoon and evening.

Chapter 36
Back at the Cottage

Some days later we find Old George recovering from his heart condition.

Friends from the village have been very good to him in collecting his provisions and newspapers. The car has been returned to the garage and repaired by a friend. The presence of two rabbits, an owl, a wagtail and a sparrow in the cottage was not a surprise to Old George's friends. He is well known in the district for his ability to befriend wildlife.

We find the old man stretched out on the settee surrounded by the war cabinet, reading the daily papers.

"Oh, here we are," said George. "There is a bit here about a scientist being attacked by animals while walking home from his laboratory."

"Where about?" asked Wagtail.

"Errr, hmm. Ah yes, it was around here. Local like. Now let's see," continued the old man. "Apparently he has had his animal licence revoked because the Home Office inspector discovered that he was being irresponsible in his research. There is a suggestion that he was cruel to some guinea pigs during studies on the chemistry of the brain."

"Sounds dreadful!" cried Sparrow.

"On going home one night he was seen to be attacked by a group of rats and guinea pigs which emerged from a wooded copse."

"Dear, dear," said 700. "What happened next?"

"He was found in a state of shock with severe lacerations to his ankles and legs. It is expected that he will have to undergo several skin-graft operations. Dear, dear me. I bet that is our friends whom we said farewell to. They always said that they could play a part in *Operation Upset*."

"And they certainly have!" stated Owl, joining in with the conversation.

Old George went on down the columns, reading about more animal attacks on villains and complaints from readers about poor TV reception and interference in programmes.

"These letters about television are certainly most interesting," said the old man. "It is surprising how many people are enjoying the absence of TV. There is one woman writing here that her home life has completely changed. Her husband takes her out a lot more and they went to the pictures for the first time in years the other day. She says here that It was like old times, queuing up to get in and buying a bag of chips on the way home. Brought back a lot of happy memories for them, it did."

"Isn't that nice," said 605, a sentimental tear dropping on to her cheek.

"Oh and here is a letter from an old-age pensioner saying that she has never had so many young people coming to the house to talk to her and to offer to take her out shopping."

"How thoughtful," said 700. "I like to hear that sort of thing."

"Yes, it is making them all think," replied George. "Though, there are some letters here from dyed-in-the-wool addicts of TV who are doing nothing but complaining."

"Can't help them all," muttered Sparrow.

"Oh crikey, I don't like this bit here," cried the old man. His colour drained from his face, even though it wasn't too obvious beneath his thick beard. His heart began to pound.

"What's up?" asked Wagtail. "You look a little agitated, George."

"I am," replied the old man. "I think they are on to us."

"Oh no!" cried 700, running beneath the table. "They aren't going to find me, I'm not here!"

"Wait a minute," said 605. "What do you mean, George?"

"Well, it says down here at the bottom of this column that the police have a lead in the Forth Bridge disaster. They think they know what type of car was used by the villains!"

"Villains! Is that what they call us? Cheek!" said an irate Sparrow.

George went on reading out loud, "The police wish to question the owner or driver of a dark-coloured pre-war car seen in the area around the time of the disaster. The police are not sure whether the vehicle was on tour at the time or whether it is local to the area. It may have been parked by tourists, as it is common for visitors to park in the area while they walk across the bridge."

"I don't like that," said Wagtail.

Old George went on, "The police are busy contacting vintage and veteran car enthusiasts. They want to question the driver of a car which has wire wheels – one of them buckled. It is thought that the buckled wheel may now be used as the spare."

"Oh crikey, George, we have had it now. They will soon have us locked up," cried Sparrow in despair.

"Yes, it does look bad," said George, trying to hide his innermost fears. "There is little we can do except lie low and hope that they do not get any further with their enquiries."

"It's worrying me too much already," shouted 700 from beneath the table. "I doubt if I can stand the strain. It looks as though I am going to get the chop after all! I would have been as well staying in the animal house. My fate is going to be the same!"

Oh what rubbish, 700," groaned 605 impatiently. "You are not dead yet. Where there is life, there is hope."

"That's very true," said Sparrow as he took a deep breath. "Let's keep our beaks up."

"And our best claws forward!" said Owl. "And our noses to the burrow!" added 605.

Chapter 37
The Fire

Old George continued reading through his newspapers while at the same time trying to forget the possibility of early arrest for his part in the demolition of the bridge. It was very difficult for him to shut it from his thoughts altogether. Every few seconds his mind would cast up the great ugly skeleton again. Turning to the sports page for some light relief he suddenly became aware of the smell of smoke.

"Is that smoke I can smell?" asked the old man, looking at Owl.

"Yes, it is. I picked it up a while ago, George, but it is coming in from outside so I didn't bother to say."

"Oh, but I think it is always a good idea to investigate a smell of burning," replied George. "Would you mind taking a look for me?"

Owl flew to the window. "It's over near Mrs Lund's."

"Oh, OK. She is probably getting the boys to tidy up her garden. I suppose they are enjoying themselves, burning the rubbish."

Old George continued reading but as time went on the smell of burning began to annoy him. "You know, that doesn't smell like rubbish from the garden," he said.

"Hmm, yes. It's rather acrid." replied his feathered friend.

Just then, the wail of a siren could be heard in the distance. The noise grew louder and louder and then stopped.

"Oh dear! There must be a serious blaze close by," exclaimed George. "I hope the boys, if it is them, haven't let the fire get out of hand."

"I'll go and see," said Owl, flying up on to the window ledge beneath the open pane of glass.

"Wait a minute, I'll go," piped up Sparrow. "The sun might hurt your eyes too much. You have been out in daylight an awful lot lately, probably too much!"

"Oh well, alright. Thank you very much," replied an appreciative Owl.

Sparrow flew up and out of the open window and soon returned in a frantic state. "It's the garage! The garage! It's on fire. The car is being burned up! Everything is ablaze."

"Good Lord!" cried Old George, sitting upright. "The car! It will be ruined!" The old man jumped up from the settee, ready to go down to the garage.

"No you don't, my man," said Owl with an air of authority. "You are not going down there in a mad rush. Your old heart won't put up with any more excitement like this. There is nothing you can do so stay put until someone comes up here. So just settle yourself."

"But I *must* go to the garage! Now, don't be silly. Let me go," cried the old man. 700, 605, Sparrow and Owl lined up in front of the front door.

"You are going to stay where you are!" said Owl in his impressively-firm tone. Old George did as he was bid, though he was like a cat on hot bricks.

"I do wish someone would call to tell me what is happening," said the worried old man.

"Now, now. I am sure someone will be along within the hour," offered Owl.

Owl had no sooner spoken when a man could be seen coming up the path to the front door.

"Who is this?" asked Old George. As the person came nearer the old man realised who it was. "Why, if it isn't Bert Cresswell!"

Old George gave Bert a wave as he came to the door. He didn't bother to wait to be invited in, he just tapped on the door and entered.

"Hello, Bert! How are you? I bet I know what you are up here for."

Bert looked a bit anxious and embarrassed. "Well, it's about the car," he said.

"Yes, I thought as much. Burnt out, is it?" asked Old George. "How did you know?"

"Well, *you* answer my question first!"

"Well aye, it is indeed burnt out," said Bert. "Nothing left but the metal frame and chassis. Almost unrecognisable, it is. But I suppose you know that as well."

"Oh, no. I only know that there was a fire, that's all."

"But how do you know that, George? You can't see the garage from here."

"Oh, err, I smelled smoke," said George. "That's what it was, I smelled smoke." He was reluctant to tell his friend about his ability to converse with Owl.

"I see," replied Bert in a doubtful voice. "It were all my fault really. I fixed the wiring as best as I could before putting the car away for you that day, but being too confident I let the battery coupled up. There must have been a short circuit somewhere and it's set the whole car on fire. This is always a worry with these old jalopies. The new plastic wiring is nice and safe but that old rubber and cotton-covered stuff is murder when it gets old and rotten. Once it starts to go you can't seem to catch up on repairs. It short circuits all the time."

"Oh, I can't blame you, Bert," said Old George as he tried to console the man. "The thing is, Bert, what happens now? What about the scrap?"

"Well we can give that to the scrap merchant over in Bedford. They'll crush it up in to a metal cube and pack it off to the steel foundry. It's all metal, you see. No plastic or fibreglass in that frame. All the combustible stuff has been burnt off. Do you want me to phone them up? I think they come round these parts tomorrow."

Old George thought hard about other rapid ways of getting rid of the old car but the more he thought about it the more he was convinced that fate had taken a turn for the better. For all intents and purposes the old Wolseley was already unrecognisable and, in a few hours, would vanish from existence. In effect this was practically a miracle of good fortune! The police would never be able to trace the vehicle. Old George realised that the plastic letters on the number plates would already be melted away, so nobody would know the registration number either. In any case, the car was still registered in the late doctor's name!

"Aye, now look Bert, get these people to collect the car today if possible, not tomorrow. The sooner the place is tidied up, the better."

"OK, George. As you wish. Well, I'll be saying my farewells. I suppose the insurance will cover you for the fire. If not, I feel obliged to compensate you," said Bert.

"Don't you worry about that," said Old George. "The car was finished, anyway."

Old George didn't really think the car had been finished at all but under these circumstances he was glad that the accidental fire had taken place.

"I'll be off then," said Bert. "Awfully sorry about events. Bye now."

"Ta ra, Bert. Be seeing you!"

Owl, 700, 605, Wagtail and Sparrow jumped up and down with glee. "What a funny world, eh George?"

"Aye it is a funny world right enough," agreed the old man. "Now let's go in to the cottage and try to forget about the fire."

After entering the cottage the old man made a cup of tea and sat down to re-scan the newspapers.

"You still reading the papers?" asked 700.

"Aye lad," replied Old George. "Just thought I might have missed something of interest."

He quickly flipped over the pages until he came to the section that covered radio programmes.

"I see here that Radio 4 are going to have a long phone-in discussion tomorrow night at eight in the evening," muttered the old man.

"What was that?" asked Sparrow.

"There is going to be an open-ended discussion on Radio 4, starting at eight o' clock tomorrow. The public are going to be invited to participate in the form of a phone- in. That should be very interesting, as recent events and animal behaviour are on the agenda."

"It sure will," said 605. "It will really indicate the effect of our actions on the general public. I bet we have made them sit up and think!"

"Roll on tomorrow night!" cried Owl.

Chapter 38
The Radio 4 Phone-in

"George, hurry up! It's almost time for the phone-in," shouted Owl.

The old man came dashing in from the kitchen with a large mug of tea in his hand. "Just made it," he exclaimed, at the same time switching on the radio.

The war cabinet made themselves snug in front of the fire.

"Brr, a bit chilly tonight! It seems that lately the ol' summers have been getting more like winters! Never used to be like this!"

"Go on with you! You are getting old!" said Wagtail.

"Aye, it could be that too," replied George as he admired the goose bumps on his arm.

"Ssssh!" bellowed 700. "The programme is about to start."

"The time is now eight PM," boomed the radio voice. "Tonight we have cancelled our usual programmes so that we can host an open-ended discussion…"

"Oh do get on with it," cried Owl. "We know this already!"

"Ssssh!" whispered Sparrow.

The radio went on, "In the studio tonight we have the Scottish Secretary of State, Mr Muggins. We are also joined by the MP for West Lothian, who happens to be a qualified vet, and by Admiral Blenkinsop-Hardlie-Nelson. We would like to take this opportunity to openly apologise to the admiral because the last time we attempted to interview him, regarding the bridge disaster, we ran short of time."

"Thank you very much," replied the admiral. "As I was going to…"

"Yes, thank you, Admiral. We must get on with the programme. Now as I was going to say, the lines are now open to the public so if I go to our switchboard, we should get our first question for tonight."

The chairman of the discussion lifted the handset. "Good evening, my name is Mrs Randle from Cheam."

"Yes, Mrs Randle. What is your question?" asked the chairman.

"I would like to know why my young son was savaged last week by an unknown group of animals and what is the government going to do about these attacks, which seem to have become commonplace in recent days?"

"I think this is a good question for our vet," said the chairman.

"Good evening, Mrs Randle. I think the answer unfortunately lies with your son. I apologise about saying this so matter-of-factly but it would appear that the animals are only attacking villains. This is a hard pill for a parent to swallow but there it is. I am not saying that I agree with the animals' actions but they have certainly done a lot of food in their approach to the problems of crime in our society. Alas, while I am an MP as well as a vet, I am not in a position to enlighten you on government action, because the government themselves do not know where to start first. You see, Mrs Randle, it is still a mystery as to how they are trained and coordinated in their actions against crime.

They may even be receiving a new drug, or it may be the result of radio waves. Who knows? I'm sorry I can't be more helpful, Mrs Randle."

"We'll have to do away with the niceties I'm afraid," interjected the chairman. "The lines are absolutely jammed with callers, so could we go on to our next questioner."

"Mr Folkeston from Wolverhampton, here. I would like to ask the vet about the law governing European pharmaceutical companies coming to Britain in order to carry out work involving animal experiments? Are these animals protected against unethical practices?"

"Yes, they are protected in the same way that all animals are protected by the Cruelty to Animals Act. Foreign scientists must apply to the Home Office for a licence, a licence which is only issued for use on specific problems on specified premises that are deemed acceptable by the Home Office. The potential licensee must be suitably qualified before the Home Office declares that, well, they *do not wish to disallow a licence.* I am aware the wording may sound ridiculous but one must remember that nobody has a right to a licence. Ordinary members of the public, for example, are automatically disallowed a licence."

Aberdour Harbour (by Hayden Jeffery MSc)

"Thank you," said the chairman. "I think we should try another subject now to keep variety in the discussion. I have a call from a Mr Spence of Ealing now."

"Hello, yes. Can Admiral Blenkinsop-Hardlie-Nelson inform us of the current situation regarding the passing of boats up the River Forth now that the bridge has been sabotaged?"

"Well now, Mr, err. What did you say?" spluttered the admiral. "What did you say your name was?"

"Mr Spence, it is. Mr Spe—" he was interrupted by a pipping noise. "Blast, just a minute while I get my money out and top up this thing."

It was too late, the call dropped out.

"Well, we seem to have lost the admiral's questioner. I think it would be impolite to go on with the admiral's question without the caller on the line. Perhaps we could have another question. Next caller?"

"Mr Rowbottom from Hampshire here. I would like to ask the Secretary of State for Scotland a question on the liquid gas plant at Mossmorran in Fife and the proposed terminal at Braefoot Bay near Aberdour and Inchcolm Island."

"Please go ahead, Mr Rowbottom," answered the politician.

"I know these waters very well from my time in the Royal Navy. Recently, we saw the sabotage of the Forth Road Bridge by unknown saboteurs. This bridge is only a few miles from Braefoot Bay. What measures are being taken to safeguard the public against similar attacks on something as volatile as a liquid gas loading terminal? Surely an explosion in these confined waters would be a disaster?"

"The government look upon the bridge disaster as an isolated instance of sabotage, so they feel that realistically there are no further safeguards necessary at Braefoot Bay. I must point out to Mr Rowbottom that I have not yet decided on whether the Braefoot project will go ahead or not."

"But this is lunacy if you don't mind me saying so, sir," retorted Mr Rowbottom. "Even if we ignore deliberate sabotage what about the risk of fire caused through a collision? The stretch of water involved is essentially a main sea lane for naval vessels and cargo vessels going up to Rosyth and Grangemouth. Furthermore, oil tankers are loaded at the jetty close to the Forth Railway Bridge. "

"Yes, but that…"

"And what's more, the area is full of pleasure sailing craft in the months from April to October," continued the vociferous caller. "These pleasure sailors are advised by the coastguard and government bodies to carry flares in case of an accident at sea. A lot of these craft now carry gas cookers and water heaters. If a flare was fired in the region of a tanker which was loading and possibly carrying liquid gas, or if a seepage of gas managed to gain access to a passing yacht, there would be an almighty explosion."

"Are you suggesting that yachtsmen cook lunch when on the move in the Forth?

Really, Mr Rowbottom."

"Don't try to evade the issue, Mr Secretary of State. It is common practice for yachtsmen to make tea and coffee while sailing up and down in these waters."

"It has already been decided that all ship movements in the region will cease when a gas tanker is being dealt with at the terminal."

"What do you mean, *dealt with*? And what do you classify under the term *ship movements*? Do you mean that all pleasure sailing will have to stop?"

"I still have to discuss the details with my advisors," answered the politician, trying not to get flustered. "I must say though, Mr Rowbottom, that the safety of the public is my prime concern."

"If you were concerned about the safety of the public you would ban development of any gas terminal in the area!"

"That is a very good point," said the chairman, stepping in. "Now, let's have another caller."

"Hello, Mr Clarkson from Dundee here. I understand that on Canvey Island in the Thames there is a liquid gas storage depot where the cold from the gas has already penetrated through the thermal insulation, causing the surrounding soil to freeze. The soil, as I understand it, is freezing outward from the tanks at the rate of six feet per year.

Surely the same sort of thing will happen at Braefoot Bay and in the soil surrounding the lengthy pipeline to the terminal?"

Inchcolm Island from Aberdour

"I understand from the oil companies that there is a remote possibility of a similar situation arising at Braefoot Bay." answered the Secretary of State.

"Then what are they going to do about it? I suppose they will demand more acreage to satisfy their greedy demands."

"I cannot answer that question at this stage. I will have to wait for full plans to be submitted."

"I have another caller who wishes to ask a question on the same subject," said the chairman.

"Good evening. I am Mr Ross from Burntisland, close to Aberdour. I am employed in the fire-fighting service and will be involved in fighting any fires which take place in the area under discussion. I am concerned about the severity of any possible fire and explosion, the reality of which will be absolutely terrifying. I am, however, also deeply concerned about the possibility of toxic fumes from the plastic industry which will follow in the wake of the construction of the ethylene-cracking plant.

"I have heard from reliable sources that on combustion certain plastics and chemicals used in the industry give off carcinogenic fumes. That is to say, they cause cancer when inhaled. A fire-fighter like myself would be placed in a very vulnerable position under such circumstances and I feel that my salary does not justify the risks to my health."

"Well, although I appreciate your concern, I think that we must accept that you have a hazardous job, Mr Ross. I can assure you that you will be provided with the best equipment available."

"If it is anything like the stuff we're issued with now, it won't be much use. Why should I risk my health at twenty-four years old? I have a wife and two children to think about. It is all very well for town councillors and the like to boast about getting extra jobs for the area but if your health suffers then nothing else matters. You see, the point is it may well be alright for me to wear an effective breathing kit, if it is ever produced, but what about the public? The fumes from a chemical fire go straight up in to the air. The public won't know what they are breathing in until it is too late."

"Oh, I am sure that we will insist on an early warning system for these plants to use in case of an emergency."

"With all due respect, Mr Secretary of State, you are out of touch with the realities of the situation. If a fire breaks out in a modern chemical or plastics factory it will be too late to warn the public. You cannot evacuate a whole town in five minutes."

"Judging from the number of calls on the line I think it would be wise to carry on with this theme of discussion for a few minutes," said the chairman. "A lot of people are terribly concerned about the environment. Could we have the next caller?"

"Hello, I am Mrs Rodgers from Plymouth. Perhaps I should direct my question at the admiral, because it relates to the weather on the Forth and he is bound to be more aware of the weather conditions at sea in such a place.

"Yes, madam, what can I do for you?" asked the admiral.

"Just answer my question and don't hedge like your colleague. I would like to know what will happen to any gas which leaks in to the Forth from Braefoot Bay, or a loaded tanker plying out of Braefoot."

"Well, Mrs Rodgers, I retire next week so I am not too interested in playing down the problem. As you say, I am familiar with the sea and also the wind. Err, what I really meant was, err, that I know the movement of air in the Forth can be extremely rapid. Now this means that in a force nine on the Beaufort…"

"Now just a minute! Don't you go waffling, admiral. I am only a common ol' housewife so just use plain language that I can understand."

"I'm terribly sorry, Mrs Rodgers. I sometimes get carried away. Don't get the chance to talk sea and weather these days. Brings a tear to my eye, it does.

"It's bringing a tear of frustration to my eye so just get on with it."

"Yes, yes, of course. Now, where was I. Oh yes, the wind can often get up to sixty to one-hundred miles per hour up the Forth. Quite often it blows from the east, although the prevailing wind is considered to be from the west. Any spillage of the dense gas would mean that the gas would flow along the surface of the sea – either towards Inchcolm, past Leither and on to the open channel or it would be blown upstream towards the Forth Bridge, North and South Queensferry and eventually on to Rosyth. On ignition, the explosion would affect all of these areas. I would not like to be crossing the bridges on the Forth when the explosion occurs. Strategically, it is ridiculous to place a liquid gas terminal at Braefoot Bay. In the event of any disaster the safety and movement of naval vessels could be severely impaired.

"In fact, the recent destruction of the road bridge stopped all movement of armoured shipping from the Rosyth base. I can only conclude that the terminal would be better sited at a more open and remote site on the North Sea. I understand that must of the gas will be exported to America anyway, so it would be sensible to have the terminal closer to the Atlantic."

The chairman moved on to the next caller.

"Mr Fleming from Clackmannan here. I was pleased to hear the word 'strategically' used by the admiral there. We are currently witnessing the construction of a nuclear-powered electricity-generation plant at Torness, near the mouth of the Forth. In addition to this hazard we have the proposed liquid gas terminal at Braefoot Bay to consider and, with the risk of boring everyone, the strategical importance of the bridges over the Forth, the Rosyth naval base, a major power station at Kincardine and the petrochemical refinery at Grangemouth. Above all, 75% of the Scottish population lives in the Central Belt. Although it is argued that the Russians, for example, would not start a nuclear war I think we must consider the potential for blackmail that the presence of a Russian – again, for example – nuclear submarine would have if it entered the North Sea and aimed its missiles at the area."

"Mr Fleming has a very good point," piped up the admiral. "I feel that his fears are very real and are shared by many of us, not only in Scotland but throughout the kingdom. The problem is, Mr Fleming, that we have allowed the population of Britain to get out of hand. The density of population, along with the construction of industrial sites, has caused large areas of intense human activity – such as the Central Belt, as you point out. We cannot really afford to disperse the population because this would mean moving on to agricultural land…"

The Secretary of State butted in, "And Britain can only provide about 45 to 60% of its food needs as it is at the moment."

Now Mr Fleming butted in," You've all made a real mess of things, haven't you?"

"I think we can all take some measure of blame, Mr Fleming. I suppose you are married with children?" asked the politician. "Yes sir. I am and I have five children."

Meanwhile, at the cottage Old George and the war cabinet were still intently listening to the broadcast.

"This is great fun isn't it, George?" asked Sparrow.

"Oh yes, it is really spreading out in to all sorts of subjects. This programme will go on for hours and hours!" came the confident reply.

"I think some of them will get so angry in the end that they will climb up the phone wires," said Wagtail.

"And belt someone!" added Owl.

"Yes, I can see that happening too, before long," said Old George. "It's rather worrying, though. Our actions have really started the ball rolling, haven't they?"

"Yes, and the lines are all jammed up with people wanting to air their views on it," said 700.

"Of course, you must remember that they do not have a television and with *The Times* newspaper out of print because of some silly dispute they are spending their evening hoping to get a word in," said George with a laugh.

"And there must be millions listening who don't have the courage to phone in," said 605.

"Or who don't have a phone in the house," added Owl.

"Tell me," asked Wagtail. "Why are people concerned about the Russians?

Remember the admiral said that the man's fears were justified, or something."

"Well," said George. "The Russians tried to build up a navy before 1939 so that they could develop the same type of naval strength that had made Britain so great in earlier times. Unfortunately for them, Hitler beat them to it and started World War Two. Hitler was defeated partly because his own navy did not have the will to fight. Oh, he had ships right enough – some very good ones in fact – but one must have support from your men. Over recent years the Russians have seized their chance to try again. They are building hundreds of submarines and under-cutting shipping prices in the merchant sector so that eventually they will rule the seas.

"They are doing nothing illegal, so nobody can stop them, and yet in the end it could spell disaster for us. Anyway, friends, it is getting late and past my bed time. I would like to continue listening to the radio but I must have my rest."

"Yes, I think you are being wise," replied Owl. "Sleep on the settee, it will save you a journey upstairs."

"Aye, it's nice and warm down here. I think I will stoke up the fire for the night and get myself settled down."

The old man put a few big lumps of coal on the fire and said goodnight to his colleagues.

Chapter 39
The Sun Sets on Operation Upset

Although the old man was very tired, he somehow could not manage to get a good night's sleep. Now and again his mind kept enlarging on the severity of his actions. As time wore on through the night things almost became unbearable, and then there was that nagging pain in his chest. Just when he thought he was rid of it, it would return. Normally he would have called in the doctor but he was getting old and knew that his time was about due.

"What could a doctor do about a tired old body?" he thought to himself. It wouldn't be worth the effort to visit the surgery. The night dragged on and on. It seemed to be endless. The coal in the fire slowly withered away like some giant about to die.

Old George thought about how a fire typifies a life in general. First the flames come in to being, they accelerate in to a full-blown and energetic life, remain steady and constant for a good while – as though everything is in balance – and then the outflow of energy exceeds the input. The fire becomes weaker and loses its energy, eventually lying quiet and dormant until it reaches the final low ebb, from where recovery becomes impossible. Death comes quietly and without much noise. If, in fact, there is any noise at all.

"There now," George said to himself. "I am getting morbid." He looked at the window and the gentle glow of light that grew as a new morning dawned. Slowly and silently, without noise or fuss, the sun came up from its nightly journey to the other side of the world.

What a tale it could tell, thought George. *If it could only speak, I bet it could say a few things about what it has seen over the many millions of years of its existence. What a mine of information the sun would be! What a pity that it is not able to record the happenings that it witnesses. Wouldn't it be good if silly old man could plug in a wire and extract knowledge at random? We could do away with libraries and listen to the sun spilling out its knowledge, or listen to the sun spilling out its knowledge, or watch the information come over in the form of television. Damn that word! No, that would be bad.*

We would be back to where we are, with more unemployment than we have now and everyone would be so lazy that they would watch TV all day in order to get the answers to their questions. Research would go on without the help of the sun because it would not hold the knowledge of the future, though it would be a good reference library for past work on the subjects being studied. Ah well, a nice dream to have. "I must get up now and stop this idle nonsense," he murmured the last bit out loud.

"What was that?" asked Owl, blinking his eyes. "Haven't you been out hunting?" asked the old man.

"No, couldn't be bothered," replied the rather bleary-eyed bird.

"You will just have to have bacon with us," said George as he made his way to the kitchen.

They all sat down to breakfast, at the same time discussing the previous night's radio programme.

"Let's get the early-morning news on," suggested 605. "They may make comment on the phone-in."

The old man got up from his chair and, still chewing his fried bread, went over to the radio and switched on. He then returned to the table to finish his breakfast.

"I think we may have missed the news," said 700. "But who knows, they may have some special coverage."

The radio came to life after the valves had heated up. The old man had never bothered to buy a transistor set for the house but he knew that he would have to, eventually. He had been told that the valves in old radios were becoming extremely difficult to obtain.

"You were right, 700! They are discussing the importance of last night's programme," observed George.

"Goody, goody!" chirped Sparrow. "We'll be able to get an idea of what we missed after we turned off."

"And of course, the way of life throughout Britain has changed dramatically," said the voice on the radio. "The absence of TV has increased the sale of beer by thirty percent. Cinema attendances are up four-hundred percent and theatres are fully-booked, as are sports centres. Vandalism and mugging has stopped, partly because of animal action but also because the streets are busier at night. In fact, the evenings have come back to life and there is a refreshing air of activity everywhere. People are realising again that friendship and conversation is so important. Old age pensioners feel safer at night because others are looking for someone to visit and help.

"We also learned last night that the Post Office services are busier, carrying more letters as people are finding the peace to sit down and write letters. Mail order companies are benefiting as well because their catalogues are being more widely read. What strange creatures we are!"

"He can say that again," said Owl. "Ssssh," hissed Sparrow.

The radio went on, "The conservationists certainly aired their views last night. We at the BBC got the impression that everyone was now a conservationist. Certainly, the appreciation of the public for animals has increased enormously. We have the impression that animals can do no wrong at all. This feeling is supported by the lobby against unnecessary use of animals in research and in the cosmetic industry. Judging by the queues outside some of the country's zoos and parks there is now a great desire amongst the public to engage with and learn more about our animal friends. Let's hope it is not just a flash in the pan or a nine-day wonder. Certainly, the sponsorship of wild animals in the zoos has multiplied several thousand times. There is not a zoo in the country which is now short of cash." The animals in the cottage were so fixed on the radio that they didn't see Old George leave the room and make a quiet exit out of the front door. After some time, Sparrow looked away from the radio and noticed that George had vanished.

"Where has he gone?" asked Sparrow. "Who?" wondered Owl.

"George."

"I don't know," replied the rest.

After a while, the radio announcer neared the end of his comments about the views expressed the previous night. People were clearly pleased, for example, that vandalism had dropped from two hundred thousand reported cases a month to almost nil. The public were pleased, too, that after research had demonstrated that high volumes of lead in petrol had been recognised as being detrimental to human health efforts were going to be made to cut back on the amount of that element in fuel. One suggestion to offset the problems removing lead would create was to introduce an amount of methanol to petrol but this in itself could potentially lead to health problems. This would need investigating, but there was an air of confidence that these things were being investigated with a view to improving human welfare.

"Well, who knows?" wondered the announcer. "We have a lot of problems to solve in our complicated lives. We only hope that last night's phone-in went some way to alleviating your fears. I'm even told that because you're all going out more often and not watching TV so much that suits are now back in demand. Denims and jeans are now out so with that in mind I am off to see my tailor! Good day to you all."

"Hey, that was great!" shouted Sparrow at the top of his voice. "I wish Old George could have heard that."

"Yes, I wonder he's got to? Let's all go and have a look," said 700.

The animals wandered all over the cottage. They looked high and low but George was not to be found. Obviously he had not returned so Sparrow and Wagtail flew off in search of him. Still, no George.

As night fell the animals began to panic.

"I'll go on a recce," said Owl tearfully. "I'll get Fox as well. We are sure to find him.

The other animals stayed in, hoping that the old man would turn up. Some hours later Owl returned with a sad look on his face.

"I can't find him. I'll have to admit defeat."

"Oh dear, I hope he is not ill," said 605.

"He may be lying somewhere," said 700 quietly. "He couldn't be…"

"Don't say any more," cried Owl. "We mustn't think these things. George is immortal, he will go on forever."

Time went by, waiting for no man – as time refuses to do – and Old George still did not appear. The days passed and became weeks. Weeks passed and became months. Summer turned in to autumn and the sky turned a pale, colder shade of blue. The wind and greyness of November came and went, as did the snows of December and January. Finally, the animals decided to go their own ways. Owl, Sparrow and Wagtail returned to their respective ways of life. 700 and 605 found a friendly warren, where they were integrated as if they had been wild all of their lives.

The old cottage lay cold and empty and the dust settled in every corner. Some of the windows cracked in the winter frost and fell to the floor in the winter winds. The dampness crept in through the unheated walls and chimney and the thatch began to deteriorate. Old George's animal friends were not able to look after the little place which had been so important to the war cabinet of *Operation Upset*.

Finally, Mother Nature took back in to her ownership what was, after all, rightfully hers. She made no big fuss about it. There was plenty of time.

What wasn't done today would probably be done tomorrow, and if it wasn't, there was always the next day.